MASTER THE GAMES THAT CAN'T BE BEAT!

The ultimate home entertainment system, Nintendo is an unrivaled source of excitement and challenge. The key to winning is discovering the codes, strategies and maneuvers that are players' most closely guarded secrets. Packed with vital information—like training tips, layout of the screen, how to score, how you can move—*How to Win at Nintendo* will put you at the top of your form!

Jeff Rovin

ST. MARTIN'S PRESS/NEW YORK

HOW TO WIN AT NINTENDO

ISBN: 0-312-91341-9   Can. ISBN: 0-312-91342-7

First St. Martin's Press mass market edition/November 1988

10 9 8 7 6 5 4 3 2

Acknowledgments

Special thanks to the following for sharing their Nintendo expertise: John Rorick, Todd Schroeder, Joey Osnoss, Chris Maher, Danny Kelleher, and Chris, Victor, and Roseanne DiFate. Most of all, thanks to Michael and Sam, who played long, long hours and died many horrible deaths . . . but found out countless secrets.

CONTENTS

Introduction		ix
One	Alpha Mission	1
Two	Arkanoid	7
Three	Balloon Fight	11
Four	Breakthru	16
Five	Castlevania	21
Six	Commando	27
Seven	Contra	31
Eight	Deadly Towers	36
Nine	Double Dribble	41
Ten	Excitebike	45
Eleven	Ghosts 'N Goblins	48
Twelve	Gradius	57
Thirteen	Ikari Warriors	62
Fourteen	Karnov	67
Fifteen	Kid Icarus	77
Sixteen	Kid-Niki	81
Seventeen	Kung Fu	86
Eighteen	The Legend of Kage	90
Nineteen	Mega Man	93
Twenty	Metroid	99
Twenty-One	Mike Tyson's Punch-Out	105
Twenty-Two	PRO Wrestling	110
Twenty-Three	Rad Racer	113
Twenty-Four	Rush 'N Attack	117
Twenty-Five	Solomon's Key	121
Twenty-Six	Spy Hunter	127
Twenty-Seven	Top Gun	132
Twenty-Eight	Urban Champion	135
Twenty-Nine	Worldrunner	138
Thirty	Zelda II—The Adventure of Link	144

INTRODUCTION

In just three years, the Nintendo Entertainment System has become the most popular toy in the country.

Toy? Did I say *toy?* Well—technically, it is. But for those of us who have been locked in combat with Mike Tyson, heard leather slap and bone crunch (usually his leather and our bone), *we* know that the NES is more. It's an arcade in our living room, a source of challenge and excitement unlike anything else in entertainment history!

It's also a status symbol. Code words, strategies, and special maneuvers are more highly coveted than Willy Wonka's Golden Tickets. How many times have friends refused to share secrets with you? No matter how much you begged and pleaded, they wouldn't tell you a thing. (Or they'd tell you the *wrong* thing, just to make you suffer!)

Well, you'll never have that problem again!

Now, *you* can be top dog. This book will teach you everything you need to know about becoming a MAN: a Master At Nintendo.

What follows are strategies on how to win at the 30 most popular Nintendo games . . . games that can be played with the basic Nintendo unit, the console and a controller.

Each game section is broken down into 20 categories. These are:

Type: What kind of game it is, such as aerial combat, martial arts, sword-and-sorcery quest.

Objective: A brief summary of the storyline.

Layout: A verbal map of what the screen looks like.

Scroll: How you move (side to side, up and down).

Hero's Powers: What you can do to your enemies.

Hero's Weaknesses: What your enemies can do to you.

About Your Enemies: The names and specific powers of each of your foes.

Menu: What kind of game variations there are.

Timer: What you're playing against (clock, running out of energy, a specific number of foes, etc.).

Scoring: What you have to decimate, defeat, or discover to earn points.

Patterns: Whether any scenery, obstacles, or characters repeat.

Beginner's Strategy: What the new player should know in order to become an advanced player.

Advanced Strategy: What the advanced player needs to know to win or improve her/his score.

Par: What the average player should be able to achieve.

NES Advantage: How the Nintendo super-joystick affects play. Note: We haven't bothered with an entry for the mega-controller, the NES Max. That one makes things *too* darn easy!

Training Tips: Things you can do to improve your performance overall.

Rating: How good *is* the game, anyway? Just in case you don't have any of the cartridges we talk about, our ratings will help you decide whether or not it's one you might want to purchase. We've used an A, B, C, D, and F scale to rate them in the following areas:

Challenge: Are you going to master the game quickly, and, if so, is it still going to give you a thrill?

Graphics: Are they state-of-the-art, or can you do better with an Etch-A-Sketch?

Sound Effects: When someone gets punched, do they moan like they *mean* it?

You'll find that many of the strategies that apply to these games can be used in other games not covered in this book (for example: if you master *Mike Tyson's Punch-Out, Ring King* isn't going to give you much trouble. The same is true for *Kung Fu* and *Karate Champ).* At the same time, we're not going to give away *every* secret to *every* game: If we did, there'd be no reason for you to play it. (This book would also weigh more than a herd of Gleeoks.) In most cases, once you get in-tune with the kinds of tricks and traps the designers have put into the programs, you'll be able to figure out the rest.

Naturally, the further you get in each game, the better your hand-eye coordination and reflexes will become. And whatever the game, those are the most important skills of all.

Enjoy!

CHAPTER ONE

ALPHA MISSION

Type: Space war.

Objective: Seven star systems in the Tetranova galaxy have waged devastating war upon one another. Exhausted, they form a temporary truce to seek out a fresh world on which to continue their battle. Naturally, they select Earth. All that stands between the alien starships, their fighters, their monsters, and victory, is you and your little SYD fighter-that-could.

Layout: You view the ship from overhead as it passes over the invaders' battlecruisers.

Scroll: SYD moves toward the top of the screen and can also dart from side to side and retreat slightly . . . though the screen scrolls inexorably toward the bottom.

Hero's Powers: Each player gets 3 SYDs per game. At the start, your vessel has tiny Laser guns, small Missiles, and moderate speed. As you fly over alien ships, you'll spot small Pyramids: Blasting these with Missiles uncovers letters, which, if you fly over them, increase your powers. The first L you nab gives you a double-Laser, the second a super-Laser (subsequent L's do nothing); the first and second M's boost your Missile strength, and S's increase your speed. If you grab a K, your ship not only jumps to the top power level, but your next SYD will start out with the powers of your present ship. Other letters: W will warp your ship ahead; F will open all Pyramids for approximately 15 seconds; and E boosts your energy by 2 units (up to 24 units). SYD also has a potent Arsenal. These are displayed on a special screen, which can be accessed when you reach 8 or more energy units, and which can be used one at a time. The Arsenal is always equipped, to start, with Octo power (the ability to fire powerful bullets in 8 directions) and a Sheeld (it protects you from bullets and collisions). As you pass over the alien vessels, you'll see red spaceship silhouettes: snatch these and you add to the Arsenal. (Note: Grabbing them doesn't *give* you those powers, it puts the powers in your Arsenal so you can use them later. Also: Powers are added to your Arsenal as you achieve certain plateaus in combat. By the time you reach the end of the second level, you will have everything there is to get. Alas, Arsenal supplies can only be used one at a time.) The other powers in the Arsenal are: Homing, a barrage that blasts open every Pyramid on the screen; Fire, a flamethrower that burns bullets, ships, Turrets on the ships, and Pyramids; Paralyser, which serves basically the same function; Nuclear Missiles, which blow the feathers off most enemies; and the awe-inspiring Thunder, which eliminates anything (including monsters) from the screen. There's also a ? symbol, which is like those mystery packages novelty companies always want to sell us: ya pays yer money and takes yer chances. For the most part the game is very generous to those who collect ?'s, most frequently giving you a full tank of E.

Hero's Weaknesses: Bullets from ships or Turrets destroy you, as do collisions. Time saps Octo, Canon (sic), Fire, and Paralyser. You lose 2 energy units for each hit your Sheeld takes, sacrifice 4 for each Nuclear Missile, and a whopping 8 for Thunder. Certain Pyramids also contain obstacles you will want to avoid: A backward K drains all your onboard weaponry, a backward E costs you 4 units of energy, and a C deprives you of both weaponry and energy. At times an R can be useful or destructive: It automatically throws you back, forcing you to refight battles you've already won. This is good if: you need more E or points or whatever; it's dicey because, though the terrain is the same as whatever you just crossed, what's inside the Pyramids often changes. It's definitely *no* fun in later stages, if you have no desire to fight squadrons you barely escaped the first time around.

About Your Enemies: There are 9 different kinds of enemy fighters: Koros 114, Ammon 006, Yakuuto 551 (missiles; a real pain to duck), 845 (it splits into 3 separate missiles), Novo 133 (approaches from behind), Metta 028 (a zigzagger), Varis, Tagami 633, and Folfu 545. The trilobite-shaped Montgande attacks alone, spitting missiles, as does the serpentine Obanon. At the end of each level you'll fight increasingly more powerful monsters: Hekaterian, Hanomaszui, Shariputra, and Bonbonera. Be warned, however, that if you don't obliterate a monster within 15 seconds, it will begin spitting heat-seeking fireballs at your ship. These are tough to avoid. The fighters and monsters (except for Hanomaszui) must be hit with Lasers or Arsenal weapons. The Turrets and Pyramids can only be destroyed with Missiles.

Menu: There is just the one-player game.

Timer: None. When you lose your 3 SYDS, the game ends.

Scoring: You earn points for everything you shoot. The squadrons of ships—those that attack in waves—earn from 50 to 300 points each. The Montgande and the Obanon net you 600 points, while the deadlier creatures are worth from 2000 to 6000 points. Pyramids and Turrets net you a measly 50 points each.

Patterns: The scenery is always the same, as are the order of arrival of monsters and alien ships, as well as their formations. But the location of some Pyramids, and their contents, occasionally varies. For example, a Canon *usually* appears in the opening moments of the first round; sometimes it does not. Sometimes you'll find an L halfway through the first screen, on the right; sometimes an S and an L. More important, now and then a Pyramid will contain something you want . . . and the next time it'll dish up something you *don't* want. Only on level one is it safe to grab everything (unless you don't want the R).

Beginner's Strategy: Believe it or not, once you master the first level, you'll get quite far in the game. To open, keep

3

your SYD dead-center, shooting Missiles ahead. This will open the first Pyramid, an F. Fall back to the bottom of the screen as you shoot the alien ships that attack. When the last one is defeated, rush ahead and grab the F. Dart right and take the S, left and scoop up the L, then lay some destruction on the Turrets ahead of you. An E Pyramid will come up on the left; approach it slowly, since the Turret in the middle (with the Canon usually beside it) will be shooting at you. Grab it, destroy the Turret, snatch the red ship silhouette, then be ready to grab the 2 or 3 E's that lie ahead, slightly to the right. If there are 3, they will be separated by a backward E: Rush ahead to the one on the right, then duck under the backward E and take the others. Hurry to the left then and capture the M, then hasten to the right and get the L or S and L which are there. By this time you will have full Laser power. (Don't worry: if you miss any of the L's, there are more on this level.) If you don't have more than 16 units of E by the time you reach the end of this phase, go to the R (the left-most Pyramid of the screen: it stands alone, or is the left-most of a pair) and head back to get more. You should have a full 24 energy units before meeting Hekaterian. To this point there has been no reason to go to your Arsenal. Although there's a Montgande at this level, near the end, it's easily destroyed with a hit to the head using your powered-up Laser; or you can simply fly around it and stay behind the Tetranovan while it spews bullets at you. (Note: If you *don't* have the full-powered Laser—the fat bullets—go to the R and return. You'll need this to fight Hekaterian.) Upon reaching the end of the level, access the Arsenal and get the Sheeld. Go to the center of the screen and start shooting your high-powered Lasers toward the top. When Hekaterian arrives, keep firing as you back down. Upon reaching the bottom of the screen, slide from side to side, ducking bullets and shooting into the creature's underbelly. It will die after 5 solid hits. Retain your Sheeld as you head into the second level. Move to the left: shoot the Pyramid on the bottom (S) and then the one above it (F). (Note: Avoid, at all costs, opening the one in the center. This is a C, and you may

4

accidentally scoot over it when the enemy arrives.) Yakuuto —homing missiles—will descend almost at once, but are easily dispatched with your full-power Laser and some fancy dancing. You can also avoid them by getting *above* them . . . though this will cause you to miss some important Pyramids. Once F opens the other Pyramids, concentrate on getting as much E as possible. At the end of the level, go to Arsenal, take up Thunder (the Sheeld will automatically return to the Arsenal, for use later), and use it to reduce Hanomaszui to quarks. (If you don't have Thunder in your Arsenal, the monster can also be slain by Nuclear Missiles. This is a tough one, though: 4 direct hits on its mouth are required to kill it—and you have 6 shots at the most. Position yourself at the top of the screen, center, and launch the first as soon as the extraterrestrial appears. Then go into a counterclockwise circling motion, orbiting the monster, firing as you come below it.

Advanced Strategy: The third level opens with the first W Pyramid (the second one, on the right), and you may want to avoid it if you're hunting for points. In any case, this is a good time to go to the Paralyser in your Arsenal. It's extremely useful against the Montgandes, which arrive one after the other. Homing Missiles are also valuable here: If all the Pyramids are open, a quick glance will tell you which ones you want while you concentrate on blasting enemy ships. And concentrate you will, since the waves come fast and furious now. It's also a good idea to pick up the ? you'll encounter here. As a rule, always go back for Thunder before you tackle the end-of-level monsters. It's the surest way to survive.

Par: 20,000 points per round is considered a modest score.

NES Advantage: Unless you feel that the joystick makes the ship more maneuverable (most players do), or you want to slow down the game to observe it, the Advantage does diddly.

Training Tips: To improve your piloting skills, concentrate on getting as far as you can *without* using Lasers as you fly over the battlecruisers. Just hit the Pyramids and collect E for the monster fight, avoiding the enemy ships without shooting them.

Rating: Requiring both strategy and dexterity, this is arguably the finest blast-the-enemy game you can buy.

Challenge: A

Graphics: B+

Sound Effects: B+

CHAPTER TWO

ARKANOID

Type: Ball-and-paddle.

Objective: The survivors of an alien invasion board the photon starship *Arkanoid* to find a new home. Instead, they're trapped by the invaders inside a huge space fortress. In order to get out, the beleaguered refugees steal the *Vaus*, a ship that looks suspiciously like a Ping-Pong paddle laid on its side, and use it to bat an "Energy Ball"—a dead ringer for a Ping-Pong ball—back and forth against the walls of the fortress, knocking them out a brick at a time.

Layout: The ship is on the bottom of the screen. The walls are above it, filling various parts of the screen.

Scroll: The *Vaus* moves from side to side. The ball bounces in all vertical and diagonal directions, but never horizontally.

Hero's Powers: Many of the alien bricks contain different-colored capsules. If the ship catches these as they fall, it obtains different powers: the ability to slow the movement of the ball (orange; a vital attribute on those levels where the ball hits certain bricks and speeds up); to catch, hold, and release the ball for better positioning (yellow/green); to split the Energy Ball into 3 separate balls (light blue); to flee one round for the next (pink); to acquire dual laser beams for blasting the bricks (red); to obtain an extra *Vaus* (gray); and to double the width of the ship (navy blue).

Hero's Weaknesses: Missing the ball as it comes back down causes the ship to be destroyed.

About the Characters: The bricks come in 10 different colors,

7

arranged in rows of the same color. All require just one hit to destroy—save for gold, which can't be shattered; and silver, which requires from 2 to 5 strikes each, depending upon the level. Obviously, it isn't necessary to destroy a gold brick to move on to the next round. They're there to make your life miserable (see Beginner's Strategy, below). There are also bits of debris from the destroyed world which drop from the top of the screen. These are easily destroyed by hits from the Energy Ball—though they also deflect the projectiles, making it difficult when you're trying to bop out the last remaining bricks on a given screen. The debris consists of conical Konerds, pyramidal Pyradoks, 3-orb Tri-Spheres, and square Opopos.

Menu: The fortress walls appear in a variety of shapes. The wall on the first level is 6 rows of 11 bricks each; the second is a staircase, 11 rows building from 1 brick on the right to 11 bricks on the left; the third is 8 rows of 11 bricks; the fourth is 2 blocks that are 14 bricks high and 14 bricks across; the fifth is a spiderlike shape; the sixth is 2 columns 6 bricks wide, 11 bricks tall, with a 7-brick bridge in the middle; the seventh is an oval 12 rows tall and 7 bricks wide in the center; the eighth has a central column 7 bricks tall with 24 impenetrable bricks scattered about (making it difficult to shatter the bricks above them); the ninth is 3 separate blocks of bricks, also with impenetrable bricks protecting many of them; and so on. There are 33 separate levels in all. The last is the enemy stronghold which fires at *you* while you shoot back at it (reminiscent of *Space Invaders*).

Timer: None.

Scoring: Different points are awarded for breaking different-colored bricks. White bricks—always the lowest row—offer the least amount of points. Yellow—always the top row—offer the most. As you move on to higher levels, the silver bricks are worth more points. Capturing capsules gives you points as well as powers, as does demolishing falling debris.

Patterns: Apart from the designs of the walls, which never change, there are no patterns. The capsules always fall from different bricks, in no particular order; likewise the debris.

8

Beginner's Strategy: The key to breaking down walls is to do as little vertical shooting as possible. Always hit the ball off the ends of your *Vaus* ship: diagonal shots take longer to reach the ground, giving you more time to get to them. It's also important to take out the bricks on the *sides* of the screen first. You can then slip your Energy Ball into that hole: This will cause the ball to bounce up and down along the length and breadth of the screen, between the top of the screen and the top row. This not only bashes a slew of bricks, but it's the high-point bricks that are destroyed. Mastering this through-the-slot technique is particularly important in order to get past those levels where there are rows of unbreakable golden bricks. On certain levels—such as level 8—it is imperative that you obtain laser power to succeed. Note: Whenever you throw the Energy Ball against the side wall, it's going to bounce *away* at the same angle. In early rounds this is the best way to blast isolated bricks. Not only will you be able to calculate your trajectory, but the Energy Ball will hit the brick, continue on toward the ceiling, then hit a side wall, giving you plenty of time to get to it.

Advanced Strategy: In order to win on later levels, it's impossible to slide your *Vaus* ship to where the Energy Ball is headed and just sit and *wait* for it. Not only will debris and bullets be raining down on you, keeping you hopping, but you'll be scooting after capsules for points and power. To succeed, you must master the use of English: dashing over to the Energy Ball at the last possible moment with a spin of the controller, *slicing* the Energy Ball rather than stopping to hit it, then rushing off to take care of the other business. In higher rounds, when the Energy Ball is coming back at you faster and faster, you can't possibly survive without this skill. Those who have earned their stripes by playing countless games of *Arkanoid* should be aware of the following: if you lose at one of the higher levels, and don't want to have to go back to the beginning, wait until the menu comes up, then tap the select button 5 times while pressing down on both the A and B buttons of controller one. Then hit the Start button. Voilà! You'll be back where you left off! Also, if you want to jump ahead to the next level, push the Start button and the A button on controller one.

Par: 700,000 points is a decent score for one trip through all 33 levels.

NES Advantage: *Arkanoid* comes with its own joystick. Using the Advantage allows you to skip ahead to screens without having to beat the one(s) before it. It also enables you to slow down the action.

Training Tips: Most players tend to grip the controller between their thumb and index finger. Don't! Practice moving the controller with the fingertips, like a safecracker. Fingertip control allows you to fine tune your movements.

Rating: This is the simplest Nintendo game to learn, though it requires great precision and hand-eye coordination to master. It is very much like one of the first of the old Atari 2600 games, *Breakout,* though the different brick layouts make it much more challenging. Visually, there's nothing here to write home about.

Challenge: B+

Graphics: C—

Sound Effects: C

CHAPTER THREE

BALLOON FIGHT

Type: Pursue and destroy.

Objective: In the one- and two-player games you are on an eerie world where Rock Islands float in the sky, evil Balloonists perch upon them, and a monster dwells in the lake. Your mission: to don a Balloon and pop those of the enemy, along with the Giant Bubbles that drift by. There are also bonus rounds where pipes spit Balloons into the air, and all you have to do is pop as many as you can before they leave the top of the screen. In Balloon Trip you must fly through the skies, popping Balloons while avoiding lightning.

Layout: Your perch and that of your opponent/partner are located on the ground, on opposite sides of the screen. The lake is between you. The Rock Islands are of all different shapes and hover at different places on each screen.

Scroll: In the one- and two-player games the screen is stationary. However, players can leave the left side of the screen and return to the screen on the right, or vice versa. (Note: On some picture tubes, usually those 19 inches and under, there may be a moment's delay as the Balloonists go out one side of the screen and enter the other. If an enemy goes out with you, your Balloonist may be broadsided while you're blind. Make sure no one's nearby when you do this side-to-side maneuver. Conversely, it's a great time to clobber the other player.) In Balloon Trip, you move from right to left.

Hero's Powers: In all games, the player moves from side to side or up and down by using the Control Button. Propulsion is provided by rapid taps on Button A. You pop Giant Bubbles by colliding with them; likewise with Parachutes and Balloons, but *only* if you are slightly above your opponent. If you are equal with them, you bounce back. If you're lower . . .

Hero's Weaknesses: If you're lower, or if they hit you from a slightly higher position, you're goin' down.

About the Characters: Only Lightning and the Fish appear in both games. Lightning drifts about the screen, vaporizing your Balloon on contact. It also is destroyed when it hits the water in all 3 games. The Fish is unpredictable: it can leap up and grab you as you fly over the lake, or it may ignore you, even if you're completely submerged. (Meaning don't give up just because you go down! Keep punching away at Button A, with your Control Button on Up.) In the one- and two-player game the Enemy Balloonists have Balloons and Parachutes: even if you pop their balloons, they can pull a ripcord and reach a Rock Island or one of the lake shores. This gives them a chance to pump up a new Balloon and attack. To make sure they're dead, you must strike the Balloon, then hit them again, this time destroying their Parachute. (If they land in the water, they're goners; the Fish'll get 'em.) The Giant Bubbles are innocuous, and Lightning cannot be destroyed. The Propeller spins on select levels, causing any airborne character who hits it to be batted off into left field.

Menu: The one- and two-player games (same screens in each), and the Balloon Trip screen.

Timer: None.

Scoring: You earn different points for popping the Balloons in any of the three games. In the one- and two-player games you also get points for ripping up Parachutes, slaughtering Bubbles, and for kicking Enemy Balloonists before they've had a chance to pump up a Balloon.

Patterns: In the one- and two-player games the Rock Islands and Enemy Balloonists are always in the same place on their respective screens; that is, level one is always the same, as is level two, and so on. On all levels you can perform certain maneuvers that are certain to attract Enemy Balloonists (see Beginner's Strategies, below). In the bonus round the Balloons come out in a different order, though there are always the same number. The Balloons and Lightning are always in the same place in Balloon Trip.

Beginner's Strategy: For the one- and two-player games: In general, the best attack is to either perch on a Rock Island or hover—and drop. Not only do you stay above danger, but you drop at a steady rate—whereas, when rising, you have to pump Button A over and over, causing you to ascend in a series of small but comparatively imprecise jerks.

On the opening level in a one-player game, go right for the island in the middle and take out 2 of the 3 Enemy Balloonists. Keep destroying the Balloon of the third; hover right above while allowing it to regenerate, then destroy it again . . . and again. Abandon this only when the Lightning has gotten too thick and you're at risk. Then go in for the kill and move on to the next screen.

There are two schools of thought about opening strategies in two-player games. Some players go right for the Balloons of their adversaries, some for the Enemy Balloonists. The wise player will concentrate exclusively on killing their foe: Not only does it eliminate the competition, it earns points. However, it's a waste of time attacking one another in the bonus rounds. Your opponent regenerates too quickly to make it worth the bother.

Whether playing alone or with someone else, if you sit your Balloonist on a perch and stay there, you'll draw the Enemy Balloonists. For instance, on level 3, if you immediately kill the Enemy Balloonist on the Rock Island in the lower left of the screen, then just sit there, the Enemy Balloonist from the lowest Rock Island in the middle will come right to you. As for the Propeller, avoid it, if possible. In Balloon Trip: Propel yourself with repeated sets of 3 gentle taps of Button A. This will make for a slow, cautious passage. Stick to just below the middle of the course as much as possible, since coasting is generally the clearest here.

Advanced Strategy: For the one- and two-player games, one of the great strategies of this adventure, and one very few players use, is throwing yourself against the Rock Islands and ricocheting into another player or an Enemy Balloonist. It takes a bit of practice to get the angles right, but it's particularly rewarding, especially when someone thinks they've got *you* on the run. Also be sure to take advantage of the pinballing effect: When there's a group of Enemy Balloonists, come at them from *above*, and you'll bounce from Balloon to Balloon, popping them all. The Propeller can be particularly useful in swatting you where you want to go, before enemies have a chance to disburse. In Balloon Trip speed ahead and get *in front* of as many Balloons as possible. Then, go back and pick them off while keeping an eye on what's scrolling in from the left. Make these dashes ahead whenever possible: it's much more effective than trying to pick off the Balloons *and* dodging the Lightning as they both approach from the left.

Par: In a one-player game you should go into the first bonus round with at least 25,000 points. By the end of the fourth round a good average is 45,000 points. As you progress, your scores should increase exponentially. Obviously, scores in a two-player game will vary, depending upon how good your opponent is and whether they attack you or your mutual enemies. In Balloon Trip, if you get through the first wave with less than 6000 points, you oughta be grounded! Hit the reset button and start again.

NES Advantage: Frankly, most players find the Control Button on the standard controller more responsive than the Advantage joystick.

Training Tips: A terrific practice routine is to play the two-player game with one player. Not only will you be attacking the enemy, but you must *also* prevent the second Balloonist from being hit. This will improve your speed and maneuverability, since you may have to race from the nether regions of the screen to save the grounded flier.

Rating: *Balloon Fight* is similar to the old arcade game *Joust* but improves on the theme with the bouncing Balloons, self-repairing Enemy Balloonists, Lightning, Fish, Propellers, and so forth. Great fun alone or with a partner, with something to offer all ages and skill levels.

Challenge: B (one-player game), B+ (two-player game), B (Balloon Trip)

Graphics: C

Sound Effects: C

CHAPTER FOUR

BREAKTHRU

Type: Military search-and-destroy.

Objective: The enemy has stolen your nation's top-secret PK430 jet fighter. You are given a super-jeep (see Hero's Powers, below) to retrieve it, and must blaze your way through the enemy to the Airfield.

Layout: The jeep passes through 5 enemy territories: Mountains, Bridges, Prairies, Cities, and the Airfield.

Scroll: Your vehicle is on the left and drives to the right. Though you always point ahead, you can play any part of the screen vertically.

Hero's Powers: Not only does your jeep shoot bullets, it has the capacity to make grand leaps over enemy trucks, bombs, landslides, water, and other obstacles. The distance and direction of a jump depends upon your speed and the position of the controller, respectively (that is, you can make broad diagonal jumps). The jeep also has the power to crush almost any enemy on which it lands—with the exception of Tanks, Bunkers, and, of course, Mines. Now and then a vehicle will come floating down on a parachute. Catch it and you acquire an extra life.

Hero's Weaknesses: Colliding with a Mine, Rock, Tank, or Bunker will revoke your license . . . permanently.

About Your Enemies: You must face 11 different kinds of live enemies. Nine of these can be shot and destroyed: Infantrymen, Armored Buggies, Jeeps, Armored Cars, Firemobiles, Missile Armored Cars, Radar Cars, Trucks, and Tanks. Two cannot be hurt: Helicopters, and any Infantrymen who are in windows. The latter fire a triangular spray of bullets; the former shoot bullets *and* homing missiles, which not only head right toward you, wherever you are, but if you manage to elude them, they turn and come *back* at you, once. There are also 10 weapons lying in wait. The ones you can shoot and eliminate are Ammunition Boxes, Drum Cans, Land Mines, Rocks that drop from cliffs, Fuel Barrels, and multi-gun Bunkers. Those that come drifting down or rocketing in at you and can only be ducked, not destroyed, are Missiles, which arrive in sets of 2 or 4, and 3 kinds of parachute-driven Power Barrels which shoot at you for varying lengths of time.

Menu: One player or two players on alternating turns can battle the computer-driven enemy. The game can be continued after you've lost your ration of 3 jeeps, though your score will not be saved.

Timer: None. There is no fuel or bullet limit.

Scoring: Points range from 100 for Ammunition Boxes, Rocks, and Mines, to 200 for Infantrymen, to 600 for Trucks and Tanks, to 1000 for Bunkers. You are awarded the same number of points for crushing an opponent as for shooting it.

Patterns: Everything repeats, from the scenery to the position of the Infantrymen, Trucks, arrival of Missiles, etc.

Beginner's Strategy: Basically, in the Mountains and Prairie stage, if you stick to the bottom of the screen, you'll be safer. (Indeed, you can make it nearly to the lake in the Prairie without firing a shot!) The Mountains are relatively easy to get through: the Infantrymen don't shoot at you in the early stages here. Seven Rocks will fall, and then you'll reach the landslide. Jump it and go to the middle, moving slowly, firing at the vehicle that will soon appear ahead. A Power Barrel will be dropping at this stage; if you remain at a crawl, it'll miss you. When you reach the second landslide, take it at the bottom and keep your foot on the gas: Missiles will be greeting you on the other side. Avoid them by scooting quickly along the cliff at the bottom and then cutting upward. Immediately afterward, line yourself up between the two Infantrymen at the bottom of the screen. Pick them off, if you want; more important, get the Truck that will soon appear between them. When you reach the Tunnel, remain just above the center of the screen and keep firing. You'll get some of the vehicles inside and will also be lined up to blast the Bunker at the other end. At the Bridge stage, stay on top. A total of 3 vehicles will appear before the first break in the span. When you reach it, *immediately* hop the divider to the lower lane. Land on the topmost vehicle, if you can; if not, land between them and keep up a steady fire. An enemy vehicle will soon appear between them. After you deep-six it, speed up. There's nothing between you and the next break in the bridge. Once you jump it, slow down: a Truck and Infantryman will have to be destroyed before you can pass. The bridge curves upward then and brings you to a line of Infantrymen. A combination of shooting and running them over will work best. When you reach the Helicopter you'll have to jump the homing missiles (unless you want to try slipping around them (see Advanced Strategy, below). After passing the chopper and reaching the tunnel, place your bottom wheels dead-center and keep firing constantly. Send the first 2 vehicles back to Detroit in pieces, then go to the bottom and shoot the third. Then it's back to the middle for the fourth vehicle. Remain there for the fifth, go to the top and take out the sixth (steering clear of the seventh, which will be shooting up from below). Then drop back to the center to show the Tank who's boss. The Prairie is easy enough until you have to leap the lake to a small island. Drive to the top and take out the Bunker by the pier (otherwise, you won't get near the lake); slow down and wait for the 4 Missiles to pass, then hit the dock running. Pull back in mid-leap so you won't overshoot the island (adjusting your course with an up or down tap on the controller so you don't land on the Mine there). When you hop off the island, come down on the bottom of the opposite shore, so you won't be shot by the Bunker. Be prepared to jump the fence that lies dead

18

ahead. You'll soon encounter another chopper: Make a diagonal beeline to the bottom right of the screen and the rockets will miss you. When you encounter the next Helicopter, you can either jump the rockets or use the maneuver cited in Advanced Strategies. In the City, stay in the top lane, then drop to the bottom after destroying the second vehicle. Go slowly now to avoid the Infantryman in the window. After his first wave of fire (that is, the first cone of bullets), speed up to avoid the second. Keep shooting all the while, since there are vehicles beyond. The second half of the City is a piece of cake: just go slowly, shooting and dodging. When you reach the Airfield, proceed at a crawl to avoid Missiles. Also, take the walls with short hops rather than energetic vaults, or you'll collide with vehicles on the other side. You can either race past or vault the rockets of the last 2 Helicopters.

Advanced Strategy: If you fancy yourself a MAN, you'll try the following to beat the first Helicopter. Place your wheels on the center divider and slow down, so your jeep is almost all the way to the left of the screen. When the first 2 homing missiles are fired, hop them, then come right back down onto the rail to avoid them as they double back. Nudge your jeep up again to avoid the next rocket, then down again, then speed ahead to avoid bullets the chopper will be firing.

Par: If you don't score at least 12,000 points per terrain, you should have been 4F.

NES Advantage: Jumping is definitely easier with the joystick; everything else is the same.

Training Tips: Don't use the jumping ability to leap the enemy. Use it only for broken bridges, fences, landslides, etc. That'll sharpen your shooting skills. Also, play against a stop watch. Try to shave seconds off your time without sacrificing points.

Rating: This game is fun, though not for the seasoned player. It becomes tedious in places once you've learned the layout and the location of the enemy. A timer would have made it more exciting, forcing you to go as quickly as possible.

Challenge: C-

Graphics: B (The jets in the hangars at the Airfield are knockouts; the landslide and bridge graphics are also very impressive. When you win, the takeoff of the PK430 is fun to watch.)

Sound Effects: B —

CHAPTER FIVE

CASTLEVANIA

Type: Horror search-and-destroy.

Objective: Because you're one brave soul, you've decided to enter the monster-infested Castlevania and slay the Evil Count. There are 6 different floors: Do you have the courage (and skill) to make your way through them all?

Layout: The eerie estate is recreated in all its dusty detail, from the main floor to the watery dungeons to the monster-infested grounds.

Scroll: The hero searches from left to right, with a limited amount of top-to-bottom play.

Hero's Powers: When you enter the creaking gates, you have only a whip, 16 power units, and modest jumping and ducking ability. As you travel along, you can obtain other weapons and defenses . . . all of which consume Hearts as they operate (see below); each new weapon you collect replaces the one you got before it. Concealed inside creatures, Candles, and/or stones, are: a Dagger (the first weapon you'll find . . . in a brazier, before you enter the house); a Boomerang; a Cross, which kills every monster on the screen; Invisibility Potion, which protects you from harm for 5 seconds; a Star-Mace, which boosts the power of your whip; bottled Fire Bombs; an Axe; a Watch, which freezes the enemy for 5 seconds (at one Heart per second); a Pork Chop, which adds some of the power you may have lost; Magic Crystals (obtainable *only* from the final creature on each floor), which restore *all* the power you lost; Double

21

Shots (II) and Triple Shots (III), which boost the effectiveness of your weapons.

Players begin the game with 10 Hearts; as you travel, you nab Small and Large Hearts, which provide 1 and 5 extra shots with each weapon, respectively. Once they're uncovered, all objects remain on the screen for 5 seconds. Don't forget to grab the Magic Crystal left behind when each end-of-level monster dies (see About Your Enemies, below). As noted earlier, these replenish *all* your lost power units.

Hero's Weaknesses: Getting struck by enemies robs the hero of one or more of his 16 power units. When they're all drained, he's dead. He also dies when he's knocked or falls off a ledge.

About Your Enemies: The house is chock full of them. At the end of each level there are increasingly more powerful foes: the Phantom Bat, Queen Medusa (these are the only two who can be affected by a Watch; see Hero's Powers, above), The Mummy Men (they fling lethal wrappings your way), the Frankenstein Monster (and Igor, who climbs from the Monster's shoulder and attacks you separately), the Grim Reaper (it hurls a rain of scythes), and, finally, the Evil Count himself. Each floor is also inhabited by lesser demons, such as Zombies, Black Leopards, Fish Men who spit fire, flying Medusae, Ravens, Bats, Eagles who drop rocks on you, Skeletons that hurl deadly bones your way, Ghosts, Hunchbacks, Axe Men, Skele-Dragons, and others. All rob the hero of endurance points; most can be slain with just a crack of the Whip, though more powerful weapons work better.

Menu: There's only the one game.

Timer: The clock, counting down in real-time, gives you more time for the more difficult levels: that is, 300 seconds for the first floor, 400 for the second, and so on.

Scoring: You earn points for killing monsters, for example: 100 for the Zombies (which are the first creatures you face), 300 for the Fish Men, 3000 for the Phantom Bat and Mummy Man, 5000 for Frankenstein, 7000 for the Grim Reaper, and a sanguinary 50,000 for the Count himself. Extra points are awarded if you slaughter 2 creatures with one use of a weapon (for example, 2 Zombies with one snap of your whip). You also get points for finding Money Bags, Treasure Chests, Crowns, and other glowing objects located inside floors, stones, or monsters.

Patterns: The house hasn't changed for centuries; it won't change from game to game. Nor will the coming of the creatures or the location of most of the weapons and goods they have to offer.

Beginner's Strategy: Whip the braziers outside the mansion: the last one will give you a Dagger. Don't go right inside the castle; jump over the door, to its right, and a bulging Money Bag will appear behind you. Get it and go in. Upon entering, kill the Zombies and watch out for the Panthers on the upper level. Whip the last block of the Panther staircase: a Money Bag is there. Before going downstairs (the steps are on the far left, set in the floor; you'll know to go there when you can't leap the gap in the above-ground staircase), head to the ground level and crack the bottom 2 blocks on the thick wall to the far right: a Pork Chop is interred there. (Be alert: a Bat will attack when you go to get it. If you whip it too soon, anything it's carrying will be frozen in the stones.) Going below, don't dawdle: the Fish Men hop from the waters quickly and in increasing numbers. If you let them collect, their fireballs will knock you into the water. If one of them *does* unleash his flaming halitosis, duck and whip him from a crouching position! Your Whip is sufficient to slay these beasts. While you're down there, you may wish to drop to the second-lowest level of blocks, on the right. Whip the last block of the ledge you were on: a Money Bag is hidden there. Drop down to the lowest block to claim it, but watch out: Fish Men will also be spilling off the ledge onto the block. Going back upstairs, make sure you obtain 2 items: the Axe (located in the Candle at the end of the last staircase, just before the Phantom Bat's room), and the Double Shot (inside the Bat room: go to the 2 blocks on the right, leap over them, and whip the one on the right). When the bat arrives, fling Axes at it: 3 shots plus a final fare-thee-well crack of the whip will send the monster down in flames.

23

On the second floor whip the Candle just above you to get the Boomerang. Climb the first staircase, stop on the ledge, hop up, and kill the Black Knight with the Boomerang. Then face right, whip the wall, and claim the Crown. Continue, and when you see a Knight standing on a ledge below you, hop onto the stone on his left, break the top block directly to your right to expose a Double Shot. Hop back up and get it. As you press on, Medusa Heads will attack in their oscilloscope-wave motion. Proceed normally —but don't hesitate to back up, whip them, or duck if you're going to collide. Two steps ahead and one step back isn't bad for this phase. If you're tired of your Boomerang, whip the Candle in the last window to get a Dagger. Use it, or your Whip, to kill the Knight(s) on the other side. (Three lashes will do it, 2 Daggers, or 1 toss of a Boomerang.) Go slowly, though, for a Treasure Chest may appear *behind* you, below the window.

When you ascend, you'll be besieged from the right by more Medusae. *These* creatures you'll *have* to whip; wait until one is waist high, whip it to death, then jump. Wait, whip the next one, then jump. When you reach the two Knights, make sure you stop at the topmost pair of rocks; there's another Pork Chop there. There's also a Watch in the Candle to the right of the first moving ledge; get it. Later, when you pass through the door on the far left you'll find another Pork Chop buried in the brick on the left side of the ledge you're on. Upon reaching the trio of Presses (the moving ceilings), use the Watch to freeze them, and run through; don't run *so* fast, though, that you pass up the Double Shot on the other side, in the bottom brick on the left. When you come to the Cannons, approach them by whipping their fireballs and inching forward until you can whip the stone heads themselves.

Venture to the top ledge . . . the lair of Queen Medusa. The best thing to do when she arrives is to use the Watch to stop her, then use your Whip on her. It will take 16 lashes to destroy her. As you start across the third floor, you can get the Fire Bombs hidden right at the beginning— though, frankly, your Whip works just as well. If you need it, also grab the Pork Chop in the second of the stone ledges overhead. Whenever you defeat a Skeleton, pass over the defeated monster posthaste; this bony breed has a nasty habit of rising, almost at once, from their own bone heap. Following the first Skeleton attack, you'll find an Axe in one of the Candles; don't pass it up, as it'll come in handy for the Mummies. When you finally do face the moldering monsters, take a hit if necessary, but get them to stand on the *same side* of the ledge. It's *much* easier to kill them together.

Advanced Strategy: As you start the fourth floor, you'll find just what you were *yearning* for: more Fish Men. Kill them as before, then get on the raft. Don't let down your guard here; those stalactites aren't just for decoration. If you don't duck, they'll club you and send you for a fatal dip in the swamp. When you reach land, the Eagles won't give you much trouble; not so the Skele-Dragons. In order to beat them (there are 3 in succession), you must act quickly: As soon as the monster's neck bends into a V shape, jump into the bottom of the V. The neck actually bends *slightly* lower than the floor, so, in essence, you'll be standing on stone, not vertebrae. Leap up at once (before the neck rises), turn and strike the creature repeatedly behind the head to kill it. In case you're power hungry, you'll find a Pork Chop in the stone where the second monster's neck was rooted. After you kill the third Skele-Dragon, you'll face Frankenstein's Monster. Keep attacking the lumbering Monster while ducking Igor and his fireballs. When the Monster dies, his manic aide perishes as well.

The fifth level is far more difficult than any of the others. Get the Fire Bombs at the onset—this works best against the Axe Men—then kill or pass underneath the leaping Hunchbacks. Look for the Triple Shot seal in the first Axe Men room, and also for the Pork Chop in the stones just before the big red gate. There's also a Pork Chop in the far right wall just before you ascend to the Grim Reaper level. When you face the Royal Axe Men (they're in the red-draped room, attending the Grim Reaper), you'll also be attacked by Medusa Heads. By this time you will have replaced the Fire Bombs with a Boomerang (found under a Dragon Skull Cannon among the Red Skeletons). Move slowly here, in spurts, firing at the Axe Men while avoiding Medusa Heads. Many of your throws will hit the Heads and Axes instead of the Axe Men. Don't worry, there are Double and Triple Shots to be found in these. When you get to the Reaper's room, go to the center and, jumping, *immediately* begin throwing your Boomerang to the right. The Reaper will descend from the ceiling on that side. Get as many hits in before the monster starts tossing scythes . . . and *you* have to start ducking and dodging. Marshaling all of the skills you've acquired to this point, head up to the sixth floor . . . and your confrontation with the Count.

Par: Racking up 30,000 points per floor is a good day's exorcism.

NES Advantage: Being able to keep the button depressed for rapid whipping is convenient, though not significantly advantageous.

Training Tips: You'll learn to master your hero's powers easily enough. The key to winning is knowing where you can find all the power boosters, Money Bags, and the like. Make your way through the house using the "Continue" mode, paying little attention to the time, just trying to uncover weapons and treasure.

Rating: Apart from being fun and challenging, and fraught with things to explore and discover, the game has incredible atmosphere and memorable monsters, as well as a chilling musical score. Some creaky sound effects would have been nice, though.

Challenge: A
Graphics: A
Sound Effects: B

CHAPTER SIX

COMMANDO

Type: Military search-and-destroy.

Objective: Super Joe's the name, and super-soldiering's the game. Helicoptered into hostile territory, your task is to kill enemy soldiers, free your comrades along the way, and collect valuable goods. And killing the foe is a tall order indeed, since they swarm, literally, like ants at a picnic.

Layout: The principal areas of combat are jungles, bridges, bunkers, an airfield, and 33 Underground Shelters.

Scroll: Joe battles his way vertically while the player watches from overhead.

Hero's Powers: Initially you're only packing a gun, 5 hand grenades, and 3 lives. (Notes about the bullets: You have unlimited firepower, though the bullets can't go through objects such as trees and bunkers—neither can those of your enemy—and only have a range of roughly one third of the screen, as compared to two thirds for your foes. Joe's gunfire will not harm his own comrades.) Scattered along the way are Ammunition Boxes, which replenish the grenade supply (3 for the first, 4 for the second, and so on); a Life Badge, a medal that adds another Joe to your bench; Super Grenades (awesomely powerful, they kill everything on the screen, but can only be used once); a Flashlight (the screen goes dark and the enemy is blind, but Joe can see); a Wireless Remote Radio, which kills everyone on the screen and gets you a chopper lift to the next level; a Medal of Honor, which bestows an extra life; Binoculars, which re-

27

veal where the Underground Shelters are; and a Bullet-Proof Jacket which can repel 10 bullets or 2 hand grenades. Also, rescuing captured soldiers can be rewarding: If Joe saves all 7 of his comrades in a specific Shelter, his grenades automatically become more powerful; if he rescues one from a different subterranean prison, his machine gun gains firepower; and if he liberates a special captive from an underground jail, one who holds up a grenade sign instead of a point value, his grenade supply will be limitless.

Hero's Weaknesses: Getting shot, hit by a vehicle, or tumbling into a trench or pond will leave Super Joe super-dead.

About Your Enemies: Many swine lurk in the killing fields. There are Foot Soldiers, Water Soldiers, Trench Soldiers, Knife Soldiers, Shield Soldiers (no . . . you can't shoot them from behind, either), Motorcycle Soldiers, Mortar Soldiers, Machinegun Soldiers, Bazooka Soldiers (hit 'em from the side), Watchtower Soldiers (ice them with a grenade), Commanders, the Leader, and Trucks, Jeeps, and Cannon Bunkers. Just to make things even more miserable, there are Snakes slithering about.

Menu: There are games for one player, for two players on alternating screens (each playing their own game), and for continuing from your last screen.

Timer: Only Super Joe's death, or completing each of the 4 levels 4-times, will stop the game.

Scoring: You get different points for killing different soldiers (starting at 150 points), for finding any power items along the way (see Hero's Powers, above), for freeing captured soldiers (1000 is your base reward; be warned, however, that once any captive is escorted by the enemy off the top of the screen, he's gone for good), and also for picking up a Money Bag (which appears when you kill using grenades), K-Rations (when you kill a sergeant by grenade), Corporal Stripes (for killing a corporal underground), Lieutenant Stripes (ditto for a lieutenant), and Gasoline Cans. You get extra points for completing a level or freeing a prisoner. See also the final note in Advanced Strategy, below.

Patterns: The screens and soldiers' approach are always the same, as are the location of Ammunition Boxes, captives, and Underground Shelters. However, other items come and go at random.

Beginner's Strategy: As you play, make a map of where every prisoner or Underground Shelter lies. For example, the first Ammunition Boxes will lie dead ahead. The first entrance to an Underground Shelter is behind the first wall. There's more Ammunition just behind the thicket of trees that stretch from the left, halfway across the screen; your first prisoner is being hog-tied by enemy thugs in the next clump of trees you'll encounter on your left. You'll find other Shelters in the right-hand wall of the first overpass, and across the third gray bridge, just beyond the wall. Ammunition is scattered at 3 points among the enemy barracks (behind the third one up, behind the first trench on the right, and behind the last building on the left). Note: Underground Shelters can only be accessed by tossing grenades behind walls, bridges, and the like. Whatever you do, once you start the second level, watch out for traffic! You will immediately be greeted by a vehicle coming down at you, followed by another rolling across the screen. Move first to the left, then up, to avoid them both. When you reach the barracks, stand beside it and cut down the soldiers as they emerge. Also, make sure you go under each overpass with your gun blazing. Wait until the Motorcycle Soldier has passed (or else he'll plug you with a grenade), then run ahead firing at the creeps on the other side.

Advanced Strategy: Several alleged pros advocate the spin-and-spray approach—constantly turning as you proceed, and firing at random, putting lead into everything that bleeds. However, this is for wimps. Constantly move ahead, watching for groups of soldiers to appear; shoot any clusters or soldiers in a row before turning on individuals. A tip for the worthy warrior: when you come to Underground Shelters where there are poles, fire at the poles. You may find an artifact worth 10,000 points!

Par: Cumulative scores for each level should be at least 60,000 (first), 90,000 (second), 120,000 (third), 200,000 (fourth), and so on. By the end of the sixteenth screen, you should be close to one million points.

NES Advantage: The Turbo factor is considerable: 2 bullets fire in succession, instead of just 1 with the normal controller, and they also reach halfway across the screen.

Training Tips: Run through the game without shooting. Just practice dodging and using the rocks, trees, and bunkers for protection. When you play a real game, these skills should be second nature.

Rating: Okay, so *Commando* glorifies wholesale carnage. But the good news is, if you get it all out of your system here—and you *will*— you'll be one peaceful dude in real life. *Commando* is different enough from *Ikari Warriors* so that you'll want to own both.

Challenge: B+

Graphics: C+

Sound Effects: C

CHAPTER SEVEN

CONTRA

Type: Military search-and-destroy.

Objective: In 1957 a UFO plowed into the Amazon basin. Today, terrified natives report that an evil entity has taken over the region. The creature—the Red Falcon—is using the conquest of Earth as the first step in a plan to take over the universe. Hoping to wipe the invader out, the Pentagon sends soldiers Lance (a.k.a. Scorpion) and Bill (a.k.a. Mad Dog) south . . . into the grotesque, alien jaws of danger.

Layout: The heroes battle their way through the space monster's 8 lines of defense: a Jungle, Base 1, a Waterfall, Base 2, the Snow Field, the Energy Zone, the Hangar Zone, and, ultimately, the Alien's Lair.

Scroll: The screen moves from side to side in all but the Bases. Here, the view is from over the soldiers' shoulders as they muscle through.

Hero's Powers: Each soldier begins with a rifle, jumping and running ability, and 3 lives; he earns a new life each time he successfully negotiates a defense zone. Soldiers can shoot Flying Capsules, Pill Box Sensors, or, in some cases, Red Guards, all of which release Falcons. These Falcons do not disappear until the hero has moved ahead and the screen has scrolled past them. (Even if you lose a life, the birds remain perched where they are.) Each Falcon is labeled and, when snatched, bestows either big-bullet Machine Gun power (M), Laser power (L), Fire Ball power (F), Rapid-Fire ability (R), the fan-of-death Spread Gun ability

(S), a Force Field (B), and Mass Destruction (it glows and kills everything in sight; sadly, it can't be stored, but explodes on contact). R, L, M, and F can't be employed simultaneously. Combined, R and S are the fighters' most formidable weapon.

Hero's Weaknesses: Getting hit with enemy projectiles, whether lead, explosives, rings of fire, etc., will end the game. Colliding with the enemy also will cause instant death, whether you're running, standing still, lying down, or jumping. Finally, the soldiers perish if they fall from a cliff (in all but the Jungle, where it's okay to go for a swim).

About Your Enemies: With the exception of the head alien and the red-garbed Royal Guard, none of the characters have "official" names. However, *you* can call them *deadly*. Among the many monsters and foes you'll fight are the elite soldiers in the Jungle and Base 1; at the end of the Waterfall, a horrible statue guards the entrance to Base 2. The bug-faced monster spits circles of fire from its mouth and from the tips of its 2 twining tentacles. There are more soldiers and Royal Guards in Base 2. In the 9th chamber of Base 2 you'll meet the Heads, creatures that divide and spit deadly homing bubbles; also ready to stomp you there are Samurai and Winged Bears, the latter of which swoop down at you. Hardware takes over in the Snow Field as you battle murderous artillery as well as crushing Battletanks with spikes on the front. However, all of these and other foes pale before the menace of the Red Falcon and its ugly larvae *and* living viscera, all of which must be destroyed.

Menu: *Contra* can be played by one or two warriors. (In the latter game, both players fight on-screen at the same time.)

Timer: None. The game is over when Lance and/or Bill buys the farm.

Scoring: You collect points for every alien emissary you slay. The game does not specify point values nor does it display the score on the action-screen. You can see what you've earned after each defense zone has been crossed.

Patterns: The scenery, location of Falcons, and approach of the enemy is always the same.

Beginner's Strategy: To win at *Contra* you must be extremely

32

adept at: a) dropping to your belly in an instant, and, b) shifting from shooting straight ahead to firing down and up (see Training Tips, below). To start, run ahead, shoot the enemy coming at you, then leap into the water. Blow away the soldier on the bottom ledge, shoot the Pill Box Sensor, then run up and grab the M—also blasting the Flying Capsule that passes. This will give you an R. The next symbol will be an S, which you should grab and hold onto (passing up remaining Falcons). When you reach the facade of Base 1 (the silver wall on the right), shoot the soldier on top, then the guns in the middle, and finally blast the bottom. Throughout the rooms you'll find herein, your tactic is simple: get to your belly when soldiers appear; kill them; rise to shoot the enemy guns; and drop again when more soldiers appear. *If you're lying flat on your belly, their bullets can't hurt you!* Whatever you do, don't touch the laser beams sizzling in front of you. Those will leave you momentarily paralyzed.

Moving ahead, stay to the left side of the Waterfall. The ledges here are almost like steps and you can literally pinwheel your way to the middle of the peak. Just before you reach the flaming bridge, shoot the two Flying Capsules that will appear. Grab the Force Field; it will last you nearly to the top. Before the tentacled statue materializes, position yourself two inches from the left of the screen and start firing overhead. You've got to shoot 3 things: the red tips of the 2 tentacles, and the monster's mouth. This will take care of the tentacle on the left. Move to the one on the right, hitting it *rapid fire* when the tip is close above your head. This will both freeze and destroy it. Move to the center and shoot at the mouth, hopping to one side or the other to avoid the middle fire-ring of the 3 it spews.

When the statue has been destroyed, move on through the 8 rooms of Base 2. The strategy here is the same as in Base 1, though you must also shoot deadly canisters as they roll toward you. This is easy: just lie on your belly and fire. At the same time, you must watch out for explosives being tossed at you. It is necessary to shift *slightly* from side to side to avoid these. Red Guards will appear in these rooms from time to time: If you've lost a soldier, and need to power-up your weapon, shoot the crimson rats and watch to see which Falcon flies from them. Don't just grab any Falcon; for example, the Fire Ball Falcon is to be avoided. It isn't nearly as useful as the Spread Gun Falcon.

When it comes time to face the Heads and Winged Bears, as well as their various armaments, again start shooting from the left. Move to the right, taking out the glowing red orb set in the wall, as well as the Samurai. Blast or simply dodge the Bears (they vanish upon reaching the floor), then concentrate on the Heads. This won't be easy: You can't just run and shoot. You also have to leap to avoid the fiery rings and Homing Bubbles. The latter stinkers come down at you and, scudding along the floor, rise again. At least you can shoot the Bubbles and destroy them; between waves of rings, position yourself under the point where the Heads unite. Stand there, blast the Bubbles, and wait for the Heads to align. It doesn't take many shots to kill them; the trick is getting quickly into position between ring falls to get those salvos off.

Advanced Strategy: For the Snow Field and beyond, *nothing* but lightning-quick reflexes will enable you to triumph. Enemy soldiers come at you from the front, back, above, and below, while, from hiding, cowards fling explosives at you. There's heavy artillery here as well (lie on your belly and shoot repeatedly at the guns to destroy them), and when you reach the icy pipes, the Battletanks will try to mash you with their spiked plates. When these juggernauts appear, stand one inch from the left; tank gunfire won't reach you there. Keep firing; the armored death machine will let you know it's just about had it by turning color shortly before it explodes. Be certain to go for the Flying Capsules and Pill Box Sensors in this defense zone: The glowing Mass Destruction Falcons begin appearing on this level, and are *trés* useful. In the Energy Zone, climb around or roll under the electric beams, since you can't zap them. When you face the hopping robot, simply shoot it repeatedly. In the Hangar phase, avoid the trident arms by advancing, stopping, advancing, and so on. Take advantage of the carts, lying or standing. When it's time to face the Red Falcon itself, shoot it in the mouth, blasting the embryo aliens and other killers. When, at last, you face the Falcon's heart, shoot the Scorpions which attack, jumping up and shooting the heart between blasts. In this phase, make sure you have more than just your rifle. Otherwise, shut off the machine and save yourself the mortification of a fast demise. If all else fails, do the following when the title-screen is on-move the joystick up, up, down, down, left, right, left, right, then hit button B, button A, and finally Start. This will give you an army of 30—count 'em—*30* men!

Par: Tough players will earn 40,000 by the time they reach the Waterfall, 95,000 by the Snow Field, and so on; you should have roughly 350,000 points by game's end.

NES Advantage: The rapid-fire function here can be a life-saver. With the regular controller you have to keep pressing the button to fire. Slow motion is also useful for studying the terrain . . . or collecting your wits when facing the Red Falcon.

Training Tips: Since enemies will not begin to attack until you pass the point where the upper ledge meets the one below it, stand on the first ledge and practice your moves, especially jumping and hitting the dirt while firing.

Rating: Though the title of the game is misleading—the soldiers are American, and the menace extraterrestrial—the game is total war in a box. There isn't a game on the market that requires more dexterity and blink-and-you're-dog-meat concentration. The graphics are a knockout—particularly the monster statue at the Waterfall and the alien ruler itself —though the audio is uninspired.

Challenge: A

Graphics: A

Sound Effects: C

CHAPTER EIGHT

DEADLY TOWERS

Type: Fantasy quest.

Objective: Young Prince Myer of the realm of Willner has a problem: The Prince of Darkness, Rubas, has erected a palace to the north and is making ready to invade. First, however, he must toll his Magic Bells and summon hordes of evil monsters. To prevent the incursion, Myer must go to Rubas's castle, enter each of the seven towers in turn, and burn them to the ground.

Layout: The game allows players to journey to each of the 10 dungeons (with roughly 200 rooms in each!), as well as to various shops and the towers themselves.

Scroll: Myer moves in all directions as he goes from chamber to chamber and tower to tower.

Hero's Powers: When he sets out, Myer has only the power to fire small, moderately powerful Short Swords at his adversaries; he cannot shoot a new sword until the previous one has struck its target or left the screen. As he explores, Myer can acquire 3 increasingly powerful Blades; 3 different Gloves; 3 kinds of Helmet; 3 varieties of Armor; and various other weapons, potions, keys, boots, necklaces (for invincibility and great strength), crystals, scrolls, and chalices. These are detailed in the game instructions. Myer also gathers Hearts and Ludder (see Scoring, below).

Hero's Weaknesses: Every time a creature hits Myer, he loses power. Lose too much, and he's dead. Different creatures sap different amounts of energy. Be wary, above all, of getting too close to where the ledges are broken. If a monster brushes by you while you're there, you'll go spinning off, regardless of how many hit points you have!

About Your Enemies: In addition to the Prince of Darkness, there are 13 (natch!) evil races: Bounders, Fire Beings, Slime Beings, Rat Beings, Devils, Fish Beings, Insect Beings, Snakes, Ghosts, Clones, Dragons, Humanoid Monsters, and Tower Bosses. The lowest-level creatures—such as Fire and Slime—are killed with just a few shots. However, it takes 20 shots from your Short Sword to kill a Dragon, Bounder, and so forth. The game instructions describe the many creatures in detail.

Menu: There is just the one quest.

Timer: None. The trek is finished when Myer runs out of power.

Scoring: There are no points, per se. By acquiring Hearts, Myer increases his hit points (up to 299); by finding Ludder, the prince can make purchases of weapons, magic, etc., at the shops. These objects only appear when Myer slays monsters. However, they do not *always* appear, and the same monsters don't necessarily leave behind the same goods. When booty does appear, it remains on the screen for only 10 seconds.

Patterns: The location of rooms and their layout never changes, and creatures are always in the same places.

Beginner's Strategy: First and foremost, remember that all creatures can be slain by repeatedly firing your sword at them. Stand as close as you can when you slash, so you can deliver the blows faster. Keep in mind, too, that while you can slay monsters—including Tower Bosses—with your basic sword, it's a good idea to get as many enchanted accoutrements as possible. Journeywise, it would take volumes to map the entire realm. However, here are directions you'll need to get to the various shops to purchase goods. What follows is not the *only* route you can take. But it'll familiarize you with the realm, and, moreover, its landmarks *must* be familiar to you if you're to find your way to the Towers.

1. Go right. Shoot the Fire creatures there, collect the booty, then double back and go through the door.

2. Shoot the demons there, collecting more power and money (you can venture to the sides if you want). Head right and enter the door *(not* the door that was above you when you first entered this catacomb).

3. In the next room go to the wall in the back. You will be magically transported to the shop. Buy whatever you can afford. (To get more potion, leave the room and reenter; the table will be restocked.) At this point you should have at least 250 hit points.

4. Return to the previous room. Go to the next door on the left and enter. Go left.

5. Enter the door on the far left (it's the second door you'll see): Kill the Dragon there, shooting while entering and *continuing* to fire. If you stop, the Dragon will incinerate you. Proceed to the room behind the dead monster.

6. Go right. (Beware the Fire creatures, particularly the one that appears as you are dealing with the 3 Bounders. Bounders take an enormous number of sword hits to slay. Keep shooting at the last one; your swords will also stop the Fire creature here.) Also make sure the Sparks don't nudge you off the broken ledges here.

7. Turn into the door on the far right. In the new room head left. Go to the door on the top, left. (Don't overshoot it; if you stand beside the left *wall,* you'll be whisked away into a *most* uninviting chamber.)

8. Travel right in the new room, to the door on the upper right.

9. Go right in the new room until you reach the stone bridge. Cross it.

10. Make a right, enter the door, and kill the Black Bux you'll find there (employing the same tactic as you used for the Dragon).

11. Upon the monster's death, stroll over to the right wall and enter the shop. Buy the Shield, Jewel, and Potion.

12. Return to the Bux room, slay it anew, and enter the new room.

13. Go left. At this point go to the third shop. This will change the adventure considerably, though, because you can't return to the point of departure (which is near the

Towers; see Advanced Strategies, below) except by traveling through numerous rooms. However, it's a heck of an adventure, so: there's a mystic passage beside a door in the back wall. Simply face the wall to the left of the door and you'll be transported to a chamber with a Black Bounder. Exit on the right, stand on the symbol in the center of the room, and—voilà!—you're in another shop.

Advanced Strategy: If you're daring (or suicidal), start the game by heading due right. After you kill the fourth Fire monster, face the far corner of the room and you'll be teleported to some very dangerous terrain. A more sensible player who is interested in a thrill will take a route to the shop in the fourth dungeon, as follows:

1. Go right, up into the door.

2. Pass the creatures here and continue up, through the top door.

3. Travel left, to the end of the chamber, and turn up into the door.

4. Kill the Dragon and go through. Cross the room to the top corner and you will be spirited, by magic, to the fourth Dungeon—a room with 4 Black Bounders.

5. Go up, into the next chamber. Then travel 5 rooms to the left. Here you will find a symbol on the floor. Stand on it and you will be teleported to a most important shop. Do some buying there, then make (and map) your way back to the room beyond the Black Bux (see Beginner's Strategy, above). When you reach it, go to the door on the far left. This will take you into a green room. Go left. Here you will find tower entrances. As you climb the stairs, you'll notice that the monsters are far more plentiful *and* determined than in the horizontal chambers. Shoot ahead of you as you climb. Make sure, however, that you don't incinerate any Tower without first exploring it thoroughly. You never know what booty will be destroyed in a conflagration!

Par: Inapplicable, since there are countless ways to approach the game and various methods of winning.

NES Advantage: Save your Ludder, it's no help.

Training Tips: What you'll need most—apart from some good maps—is the knack for shooting the fast-moving monsters. When you enter a room, if you can't fire quickly and accurately, you'll be drained of hit-points in an instant. Don't play for gain early on, just enter rooms and practice stabbing creatures to death.

Rating: The most complicated of all Nintendo games, *Deadly Towers* will provide *months* of entertainment . . . and frustration. It's very easy to die in this game. Though the graphics are weak, the musical themes for each level are entrancing!

Challenge: A

Graphics: D+

Sound Effects: A

CHAPTER NINE

DOUBLE DRIBBLE

Type: Basketball game.

Objective: With 5 players on each team, and 4 periods of play, you must score more buckets than your opponent.

Layout: The screen is a full-court basketball arena, complete with cheering crowd, half-time "entertainment," team mascots, an organist, and even "The Star-Spangled Banner."

Scroll: The screen moves from side to side, as the players do.

Hero's Powers: Your players have all the abilities of a real hoopster: dribbling, passing, jumpshots, and stealing the ball—not to mention dunks, such as a standard dunk, back dunk, and one-hander. (You can only do these when you go in for a lay-up, unopposed.) Moreover, each team has its specialties. The Boston Frogs (green) make precision jumpshots and are demons on offense. The Los Angeles Breakers (blue) display TNTeamwork. The Chicago Ox (red) are extremely aggressive—they'll steal you blind—and tend to hit shots from the corners. And the New York Eagles (white) are fast as well as accurate, sinking 3-pointers more often than the other teams.

Hero's Weaknesses: Having the ball stolen, missing a shot, stepping out-of-bounds or throwing the ball away, fouling another player (pushing or blocking), traveling (jumping without releasing the ball), failing to inbound the ball within 24 seconds, not getting the ball across the midcourt line in 10 seconds, and holding the ball for 5 seconds without dribbling. Your players can also run into the backboard,

41

and though they won't be hurt, they sure as spit won't make the shot. Another problem area is pressing the B button from beyond midcourt. Not only is it unlikely that you'll make the basket, but it's very difficult for a teammate to retrieve the ball.

About Your Enemies: If you're playing the computer team, CPU (Central Processing Unit), they are naggingly adept at stealing and making baskets. The higher the level, the more skilled they become.

Menu: A player can challenge the computer on easy, medium, and difficult levels, or players can battle one another. In any case, you can select your team (except for Boston when you tackle the CPU), as well as the time limit for each period.

Timer: You can choose 5, 10, 20, or 30 minute periods. Time in the game is half that of real time; that is, the 5-minute period is only 2 1/2 minutes.

Scoring: You earn 3 points for every shot taken outside the 3-point line, and 2 points for shots from inside. Note: If you take a 3-point jumpshot but don't release the ball until your feet have crossed the line, you're only going to get 2 points for the bucket. Nor are there extra points for beautifully executed dunks.

Patterns: The players return to their positions after each period; get the ball under their own backboard when the other team scores; and always take the ball out from a few points *near* where it went out of bounds.

Beginner's Strategy: For starters, don't be the first one up in the center circle for the jump ball. Jump a moment after your adversary (including the computer), and you'll get the ball. As a rule, it may not be slick, but it works: on defense, keep slapping the A and B buttons simultaneously. The B button ensures that the player nearest the ball will be eligible to steal it, while the A button enables him to do so. Be sure, though, to lift your finger from the B button as soon as you have the ball. Otherwise you'll automatically throw it. Again, on defense, as soon as the opposing player crosses the midcourt line, start moving one of your players toward him, from under the basket. This leaves you vulnerable to a pass, but it also forces your opponent to both make that pass and shoot quickly. Better that than letting him get under the hoop: the game doesn't let you stuff your opponent as well as you might like. Be alert, too, to whoever is flashing when the other team takes the ball in. If you steal it this close to your opponent's basket, it's an easy 2 points. When *you're* inbounding the ball, switch flashing players at the last second to keep your adversary off-balance. On offense shoot from the X markers on the court whenever possible. If you're taking a 3-point shot, release the B button when the player is on the way *down*. You'll get more distance that way. On the dunks, shooting close to the basket will let you make a standard, 2-handed dunk; jumping higher allows you to do a 1-hander; and actually getting just under the basket will produce a back dunk. Pay close attention to the sounds: a swish, and you can rest easy. A clang means the ball has hit the rim and you'd better be prepared to get the rebound. Also be ready to go in for the rebound after the second of any free throws (yours as well as that of your opponent). As for passing—again, it isn't like real life, but it works. When you have the ball, keep the A button down, and the controller pointed toward the basket. You'll literally *rocket* the ball ahead. Even if your opponent is watching for this, there's little anyone can do to stop you. Keep an eye on the timer; you can use it to your advantage. If you're far ahead, eat up the clock by passing, dribbling, or waiting until the last possible moment to take the ball in. As the warning buzzer sounds, meaning that the period is about to end, race toward the basket and shoot from wherever you are. Better to try and get the bucket than to eat the ball. Finally, make sure you are in position, under the basket, to get the rebounds.

Advanced Strategy: When playing the computer—especially on level three—watch for the steals. The CPUs are pros. Keep the ball moving, passing to any player who isn't near one of the CPU players. If you hold onto the ball, or if you let your opponent run up beside you, you're gonna lose it. Among teams that you can use against CPU, Chicago will give you the surest chance of victory.

Par: Winning. In all fairness to the average player, if you come within 10 points of the computer on level three, you're doing very well.

NES Advantage: The joystick is better than the controller for the precise movement of players.

Training Tips: Play a 2-player game with just one team. That will allow you to study positions and to try out your own shots. With practice, hitting 3-pointers is actually as easy as doing a lay-up. Also, challenge the computer on the third level. You'll be blanked for a while, but you'll accomplish two things (apart from learning humility): you'll see what kinds of moves win a game, and you'll practice shooting and passing under extreme pressure. Also, try various teams against CPU to polish different skills.

Rating: Not only is the game fun for the family, but the graphics and sound effects are *spectacular*. Particularly noteworthy: the squeaking of the sneakers, and the way the screen cuts to a beautifully realized closeup whenever a player goes in for a dunk. (By the way: just how involving *is* the game? Notice that when players go for 3-pointers, they *tilt* the controller in the direction of the basket, as though that'll help the ball travel farther. . . .)

Challenge: A
Graphics: A
Sound Effects: A+

CHAPTER TEN

EXCITEBIKE

Type: Motocross race and obstacle course.

Objective: Welcome to the most treacherous set of race courses in the world! Alone, or against 4 other bikers, you must leap Hurdles, avoid Mud, and make it to the finish line.

Layout: The 4-lane course and its obstacles—as well as an isolated camera operator—are all you see as you speed past.

Scroll: The rider moves from left to right, with limited up and down mobility.

Hero's Powers: The biker is able to steer, to accelerate, to use a Turbo-boost, to switch lanes, and to shift the bike in mid-jump in order to take a landing on the back or front wheel. There are also "Cool Zone" marks (they resemble officer's stripes) which take the heat off your Turbo (see Hero's Weaknesses).

Hero's Weaknesses: The biker cannot shift lanes in the middle of a jump, can be totaled by a bad landing or going too quickly over a roadbump, and can be upended by another racer. What's more, overuse of Turbo will cause the player's engine to overheat and will result in a 4-second trip to the sidelines to chill out. Mud (the circular patches, or big stretches between sections of track) will slow the racer down considerably.

About Your Enemies: There are 12 different Hurdles, ranging from roadbumps to massive, 2-tier obstacles. You'll also find that 4 lanes suddenly become 2 or end abruptly in a long stretch of Mud. Mud also appears as small patches on alternating lanes.

Menu: There are 5 courses of increasing difficulty, which you can race alone or with other bikers, all of which are controlled by the computer. (Though 3 other racers are with you at the starting line, a few dozen have joined the fray by the time you reach the second obstacle!) There is also a blank course which you can populate with any obstacles you wish, in any order you desire.

Timer: The clock times your run in real time. (The worst possible time is 9 minutes.)

Scoring: There are no points, merely time-penalties for overheating or taking a spill. Regarding the latter: it takes longer for you to get back on, depending upon how fast you were going at the time of your demise (the average time elapsed is 2 seconds to crash and one second to get back up to speed). Also, if you fall on your way *up* an obstacle, your bike keeps rolling until you reach the ground. That can eat as much as 3 seconds more!

Patterns: The courses, as well as the location and types of obstacles, are always the same from game to game. In the multibike games, the actions of the other riders always varies.

Beginner's Strategy: To start each course, shift from the lane you're in to the following lanes in order to avoid Mud puddles or to hit ramps precisely: 1) second lane up, 2) third lane up (to clear the Mud puddles), 3) second lane up (so you can weave around the speed bumps), 4) third or fourth lane up (in order to reach the upper ramp), and 5) third lane up (to avoid the Mud). As a rule, if you come out of a leap with your front tire pointing past the five o'clock position, you're going to take a spill. Conversely, since you slow when you pull back, push your bike to the five o'clock position until the last possible moment, *then* put on the brakes. After taking a jump, you also have the option of *immediately* going into a back-wheel-down mode. That will keep you safe, but it will really take the wind out of your sails. In either case, hit the ramps and hurdles at top speed. Beware, though, when there are 4 hurdles in a row. Hit the first full-throttle, but then jerk *back* so that you land on the *down* slope of the second hurdle. Don't take your finger off the accelerator: as soon as you land, throw the controller forward and roar up the last pair of obstacles.

Advanced Strategy: The most difficult hurdles in any of the courses are the 2-tier monoliths and the second-story ramps. To get up the former, come at it fast, land on the top level with your back wheel, then rocket off, pulling out of the dive when your front wheel reaches that five o'clock position. For the second-story ramps, getting up is no problem. When you're up there, though, give a burst of gas and then get up on your back tire for the jump. Otherwise, your speed and angle of descent will be so severe that you're certain to wreck upon landing.

Par: Courses 1 and 2 can be completed in approximately 50 seconds. Course 3 should take one minute, and courses 4 and 5 no more than one minute 5 seconds. If you're racing with other bikers, courses 1 and 2 shouldn't take any longer; add 5 seconds for 3 and 10 seconds to 4 and 5.

NES Advantage: To tell you the road-rippin' truth, Advantage is a *dis*advantage in this game. It's much easier to control your bike if you lay your thumb across the controller and use it to nurse your wheels into and out of jumps.

Training Tips: Clearly, the build-your-own race course mode is ideal for practicing jumps, weaving between Mud puddles, and gauging what kind of distance Turbo adds to your leaps.

Rating: This is a relatively easy and uncomplicated game for seasoned players. However, it's ideal for young video gamers or novices.
Challenge: B—
Graphics: B
Sound Effects: B—

CHAPTER ELEVEN

GHOSTS 'N GOBLINS

Type: Horror search-and-destroy.

Objective: Your name is Arthur and you're a knight. Whilst you are picnicking with the Princess, a demon swoops from the sky and spirits her away. Hurrying after them, you must pass through 7 Gates and fight the Devil himself in order to save her.

Layout: The screen shows each of the 7 stages through which Arthur must pass: the Graveyard and Woods, the Ghost Town, the Underground Route to the Castle, the Castle, the Underworld, and Lucifer's Chamber.

Scroll: Arthur moves from side to side or up and down, depending upon the phase of gameplay.

Hero's Powers: Arthur comes equipped with Armor, a weapon (usually a Javelin), 3 lives, and the ability to leap or crouch. (If he jumps from atop a tombstone in the first level, he'll go farther.) As he travels, Arthur can exchange his weapon for any other one he finds. (If you don't want to make the swap, simply jump over the weapon.) These arms are Javelins, Swords (faster than Javelins), Axes, Crosses (they halt any attack pronto), and Torches, which not only burn whatever they touch, but also temporarily create a wall of fire). Many monsters also cart along Jars which, if slain, they leave behind; in them may be Armor, a Helmet (a.k.a. Extend, which adds a life), and a dark Time Disc (it increases one's lifespan). Finally, whenever Arthur slays a gatekeeper, a Key falls from the sky. Retrieve it and it restores Armor

Arthur may have lost, and also allows him to proceed to the next level.

Hero's Weaknesses: Being touched by a foe or projectile will cost Arthur his Armor; being touched or hit a second time costs a life. Falling from a cliff or ledge, just once, will kill the knight. He can also become a frog (see About Your Enemies). An object that Arthur must avoid is the light Time Disc (it decreases his lifespan).

About Your Enemies: There are countless demons, including Zombies, Ravens, Green Monsters that spit fireballs, Flying Knights, Forest Ghosts with their spears, and others. The toughest of the monsters are the Red Devils, which fly and breathe balls of flame; the towering, hopping Unicorn (actually a Cyclops); the Big Men; the Dragon; Satan; and the two-mouthed Devil, each mouth exhaling death. Also found in numerous places are the Magician and the Frog King, both of whom will turn Arthur into a Frog, whose sole power is hopping. (If you happen to toss fire on the second tombstone of the first level, the Magician will usually appear.) The Frog will become Arthur again after 10 seconds, or when hit by a monster.

Menu: There are one- and two-player games (separate games for alternating players).

Timer: The player has 2 minutes to get through the Graveyard, 2 to pass through the Woods, 2 to negotiate the first part of the Ghost Town, 3 to make it through the building of the Big Men, and so on. The more difficult the level of play, the more time you have.

Scoring: Arthur earns points for killing monsters, from 100 for Ravens to 10,000 for the Devil. Points are also awarded for finding the Magician and also the Yashichi, a disklike object worth a substantial 5000 points.

Patterns: The landscape is always the same, though the monsters vary. For instance, Green Monsters, Ravens, and Flying Knights are always in the same place; Zombies and Forest Ghosts pop up in the same general area, but in different places. Weapons are found all over the place.

Beginner's Strategy: To begin with, if you open the game with a Torch, start over. It may not be sporting, but it's practical: compared to cold steel, fire is slow and useless. In general, follow this rule: whatever the level, keep moving ahead as swiftly as possible, turning to kill monsters behind you *only* when they're about to strike. Stopping and presenting your back to the enemies in front will only invite them to cluster—meaning that you have more foes to fight when you continue ahead. The one exception are the Zombies. It's easy enough to turn and shoot the one undead who is usually lumbering up behind you. If you can't, just outrun it: Zombies quickly sink back into the earth. Climb the ladder to the upper level and kill the Green Monster. (If you've climbed too slowly, it'll adjust its aim and shoot at you. Jump its bullets.) Keep firing. You'll blast the Raven while it's still offscreen. As soon as you jump the third tombstone on the ridge, shoot the second Green Monster. Don't bother climbing down; if there are no Zombies below, just jump. (If you elected to stay below, you can avoid the projectiles of the first Green Monster by hugging the tombstone while you shoot Zombies. Keep in mind, though, that any time you crouch, the headstone *may* block your shot. It does not, however, impede monsters.) When you see the Red Devil, shoot it. When it rises, plug the Raven behind it. Hurry to the left so the Devil will miss you when it dives. When it rises, rush to the right. The Devil will then sweep along the ground at you—briefly, but giving you enough time to shoot it. It should take no more than 3 shots to destroy the beast.

After you cross the water and reach the woods, 2 or 3 waves of Flying Knights will come at you. Though you can kill them from behind (their shields protect them in front), it's best to avoid them altogether. Do so thusly: when you arrive, crouch at once in the middle of the tree right before the ledge. The Knights will fly by without hurting you (turn and shoot one or two, if you wish). Rise at once, cross the small island, and crouch again in the clearing between the trees. The next wave will also pass you by. Hurry ahead. If a third wave comes, crouch at the next tree in front of you. When the Knights are gone, race ahead, shooting. That will take care of the Green Monster. After its death, Forest

Ghosts will materialize. As with the Zombies, continue ahead as fast as possible, shooting the specters in front, turning to fire at low-flying ones if they're on your tail. (When you get good, you can jump and shoot them, front and back. But this slows you down and invites more than the deadly clustering: the latter Ghosts start chucking spears *both* vertically and horizontally.)

When you reach the Unicorn, shoot at it instantly. The big guy will toss fireballs and leap high into the air. Duck the flaming death, run under the Unicorn's feet, stand at the far right and fire to your left. The giant will die relatively quickly. Catch the Key when it falls. When you go through the Gate, wait until the Blue Demon appears on the right. Hop up (not *onto* the next ledge; just jump in place), shoot it, then go to the far right of the ledge you're on. Face left, and when the next Blue Demon drops down at you, shoot it. Jump to the second ledge, then the third. If you run at once to the moving platform, you can get to it before the Green Monster above you begins to fire. If you choose, instead, to turn to the left to shoot the third Blue Demon before leaping onto the moving platform, you'll have to dodge one or two shots from the Green Monster above. Ride the platform up, kill the Green beast, then take a *mighty* leap onto the second of the moving platforms. You must jump as far as possible onto the right side of this platform. It will descend very quickly, and, if you haven't jumped to shore, will carry you into the water . . . and your death.

Upon reaching the first building of the Ghost Town, wait a second (the time it takes to fire two shots of your weapon). There are Petite Devils ahead, who will come at you from the windows; the delay throws them off, allowing Arthur to pass unscathed *most* of the time. Again, get through quickly or you'll have a mess o' demons to fight. Leap the water and hurry up the ladder. In this phase you must follow a very precise pattern in order to get over and around the walls that block each floor. Shoot the Raven (it usually approaches from the right), then move an inch to the right and kill the Big Man there by firing at him repeatedly.

51

(Note: If you move *more* than an inch to the right, the Big Man on the level above will drop debris square on your noggin.) At this point do one of two things. You can run to the wall on the far right, wait until the Big Man on the other side arrives, then shoot him *through* the wall (he can't reach you, obviously), then scurry up the ladder and shoot the Big Man on the other side of *that* wall. (Don't start shooting and then abort before either monster is dead; it will hurl debris at you, which *can* pass through the wall!) The advantage to this tack is that when you get to the right side of the mansion, it will be ogre-free. The *bad* news is that you have to fight your way through the Big Men who will have used the time to herd to your left. Thus, I favor a different approach.

After climbing the first ladder and killing the Big Man to your right, go past him to the last ladder before the wall. Ascend, go left, and climb the first ladder you encounter. You're now on the fourth floor. Go right. You will have had to fight two Big Men along the way, but your ascent will have been so rapid, they won't have had time to get too close. Thus, you'll have more than enough time to kill them. On the fourth floor, turn right. Go down the last ladder, to the third floor, and kill the Big Man here. He, and the next one you must face, are the monsters you *would* have killed had you shot through the walls when you first arrived. However, dispatching them is so easy, that killing them first simply isn't worth all the other trouble it brings. There's plenty of time to shoot the Big Man here (be prepared, though, for a Raven attack). If, however, the giant is *waiting* for you at the foot of the ladder, simply pace the floor above, to the ends of the screen if necessary, until he detects your presence and is lured away. After you've killed this Big Man, descend the ladder to the second floor. Repeat the procedure, if necessary (again, watching out for a Raven).

There is no monster on the first floor, leaving you free to continue. Nail the Raven(s) that attack as you head for the moving walkways. The key to getting through this phase is to jump as soon as you reach the platforms. For example, if you don't get on the initial set of walkways before they rise for the first time, you'll have Ravens to battle. Don't think; just jump as soon as you get there, and jump off just as quickly. Don't be afraid, you can leap as far *down* as you want, as long as you land on solid ground. When you get skillful at this level, you can actually leap *over* the second of the two walkways in each set. Upon reaching the twin Unicorns that guard the next gate, shoot at the first of them, then get under its feet when it jumps. Face left and kill it, ducking the fireballs of the second (who is to your right). When the first dies, shoot the second at once, before he leaps. If you can't, get under it when it jumps, face left and destroy it.

Advanced Strategy: When you enter the next level, Bats will descend in a wave, from right to left. Shoot the first three on the right, move into the space they vacated, and shoot the ones on the left (also blasting Zombies). Go to the upper ledge (less blue-ball-breathing mountains here), fire repeatedly at the mountain you do encounter as soon as it appears on the right side (6 shots will do the trick), then put a pair of shots into the Red Devil on the steps. As soon as you fire at him, dart to the left, jump down to the lower step, and, when the Devil passes overhead, run to the right. Turn left and, jumping before it swoops down at you, blow it to crimson atoms. Don't even bother with the next Forest Ghost that chases you (it won't touch you). When you reach the next ball-breathing mountain, stop in the middle of the step below it. Hop up, pump 2 shots into it, wait for the blue ball to pass overhead (it won't drop down on you), jump again, shoot the Forest Ghost if it's emerged, and keep firing until the mountain explodes. Deal with the next Red Devil by shooting twice, racing under it to the right, turning and blasting it. Continue along the stone staircase, watching out for the Petite Devils which will attack when you reach the Money Bags. (Note: Though there are many ways to proceed, you will face Red Devils on every route. The *best* way to go is to ascend the second ladder you encounter; there's one less Red Devil along this path.) When you reach the top of the cliff, jump *all* the way down. Kill the Red Devils there (they are easier to slay than their brethren) and battle the Dragon. Blast its stinging tail segments before turning on its head. Do this by jumping up and shooting, then running under it as it sweeps from one side to the other. When only the head is left, you may have to leap it rather than run beneath it, since it'll be quite low by this point.

The fourth level is much simpler. Faced with the moving Eyeball Clouds, ascend, using them like ladders; don't be distracted by the fact that they're shifting from side to side. Battle the Red Devil on the rope bridge (a cinch; you've got plenty of level ground on which to maneuver), watch out for the frog spell and ignore the bulk of the Blue Demons as you forge ahead, otherwise you'll run smack into sprays of bubbling lava. When you encounter the second Red Devil, stay to the left and keep shooting at it. When you face the Dragon, deal with it as you did on the previous level. Your next stop will find you facing bullet-spitting Blue Devils: These you *can't* ignore, or they'll kill you. Shoot them, and also plug the Skulls on the ground. If you leave them there, they'll grow into hopping (and hopping mad!) Skeletons. Climb the last ladder on the left, go up the ladder to your immediate left, head left and jump the gap, continue left, and scurry up the ladder at the extreme left. Go right now and kill the Red Devil. (Note: An Axe often materializes on this level. It's slow-moving, but powerful.) Extra Armor usually appears at the top ledge—by which time you'll need it. Satan appears here, and unless you're both an ace with your weapons *and* very lucky, you're gonna die.

Getting through this level, you'll find yourself in a real toughie. Once more you have to climb . . . despite the fact that some very strong enemies have a different idea. Shoot the Skulls again, then head up to the Unicorn. Stay on the right; if you keep up a relentless barrage, he usually will not venture toward you. If he does, you can slide under him when he hops . . . though he'll jump back to the left *very* quickly. When the Unicorn vaporizes, climb and face your most hideous foe to date, the most powerful Dragon of them all. The creature lies coiled on an upper ledge and awakes when you're below it. Fight it as you did the others, though you'll have to determine which vantage point is best for you: you can jump up into the highest niche on the far right side, 2 levels below it, and shoot from there (dangerous); you can climb to the level below it, rush to the right, then dash to the left when it passes over you, repeating this process several times until just the head remains, then jumping the head while shooting it (this works best); or you can climb the ladder beneath the monster, speed up when it uncoils, and fight it while ascending (this one's fun . . . but difficult).

In any case, when you finally get past Lucifer's many guards and face the honcho, you're in for a surprise. Unless you have the Cross, you're going to have to attack him (futilely) with whatever's at hand. After just a few shots, the beast will appear to die. In fact, he is not dead; he was just an illusion. And you, hearty Knight, will be flung right back to the beginning of the game.

Par: This tends to be a relatively low-scoring game, especially if you choose to race ahead of Zombies, Forest Ghosts, Petite Devils, etc., without killing them. A moderate killing spree will earn you 7000 to 10,000 points per stage (that is, Graveyard, Woods, Blue Devil Ghost Town, Big Men Building, etc.).

NES Advantage: The turboing of your weapon is *very* useful.

Training Tips: Believe it or not, most of the basic skills you'll need can be honed in just the Graveyard and Forest levels. Stay there and take chances; learn what Arthur can do. Go to the Forest Ghosts and *let* them haunt you en masse. If you can shoot them all down, you're going to give the Devil a run for his money. If you have the Advantage, go through the game at least once in Slow. If you're *really* ambitious, hop right to the later levels and try your skills there. You can do this by manipulating the controls as follows: when the title screen comes on at the beginning, jab the B button 3 times while *simultaneously* pressing the controller to the right. Tap the controller on the up side, let it go, then hit the B button 3 more times. Press the controller left, lift your finger, hit B 3 times, press the controller down, lift your finger, hit B 3 more times, then tap Start. After the life-number indicator appears, the screen will read Stage 1 A. Use the A button to advance to the phase of play you want. If you go too far, back up using the B button. (Note: This code has been published elsewhere with erroneous directions. *This* is the correct way to input it.)

Rating: An extremely difficult game, requiring unprecedented coordination, *Ghosts 'N Goblins* is *not* for beginners. At times—like the 900th time you try to get through the Big Men Building—it's as much fun as having your gums tattooed. But you can't say you don't get your money's worth. . . .

Challenge: A+

Graphics: B+

Sound Effects: B

CHAPTER TWELVE

GRADIUS

Type: Space war.

Objective: The nefarious extraterrestrial Bacterions have declared war on the peaceful world of Gradius. Aboard the fleet spaceship Warp Rattler, you must fly to the Bacterion superfortress Xaerous and destroy the enemy.

Layout: There are 7 different "Stages" through which you must pass before reaching the superfortress. These are: Open Space, in which you battle alien ships; the Volcanic Stage, where you dodge huge, red-hot stones flung from the twin craters; the Stonehenge Stage, a fighter base built from asteroids; the Inverted Volcano Stage, where up and down have been switched; the Moai Stage, where Easter Island-like heads conceal ion guns; the Antennoid Stage (see About the Characters, below); the Amoeboid Stage (see About the Characters); and, finally, the Superfortress Stage.

Scroll: Left to right.

Hero's Powers: Your Warp Rattler can move in any direction and can speed up or slow down at will. It fires projectiles from a nose cannon; these armaments can be abetted each time you capture one of the enemy's golden Power Capsules, which are all that's left after you obliterate an enemy squadron or important ship. The "power boosts" you can make as you gather Capsules are: greater speed (for one Capsule); missiles (for two Capsules; these are bombs that fall and rocket along the ground); double projectiles (for three; projectiles that fire diagonally, each time you use the nose cannon); laser blasts (for four; these replace the nose projectiles and have a greater range and speed); the creation of up to two "options" or "ghost ships" (for five; they fly beside your ship and do everything you do); and a ? or force field/shield (for six). There are also very rare blue Power Capsules. Snatch one and every alien ship on the screen with you automatically becomes history.

Hero's Weaknesses: Hits from Bacterion projectiles and collisions with enemy ships—with the rocks that line the top of the screen, with the ground, or with any of the asteroids you usually notice after you've plowed into them.

About the Characters: The only living creatures on display are the Antennoids and the Amoeboids. The Antennoids are huge, tentacled orbs that drift through space and shoot poison pellets. The Amoeboids are relentless, bloblike carnivores. As for the Bacterions (never shown), they aren't terribly good pilots. However, their sheer force of numbers more than compensates for their predictable flight patterns. There are many kinds of Bacterion ships and automatons in the game: the Fan (a patrol ship), the Rugurr (a fighter), the Garrun (a pursuit ship), the Dakker (ground-based cannon), the Jumper (a leaping, ground-based robot), the Dai #01 (a more powerful Dakker), the Zab (a mine), the Foss (a cruiser), the Rashe (a fighter formation), the Venus (a reconnaissance ship), the Uska (a communications ship), the Tild (a "midget" ship), the Mazar (a "mid-sized" ship), the Dagoom (a hangar), and the monstrously huge Big Core Fighter.

Menu: One-player game, two-player game. No variations.

Timer: None.

Scoring: Each ship or creature has a different point value.

Patterns: Every vessel and being has its own distinctive motion. For example, the Fans always travel in squadrons of 4, moving in a line and peeling off at your Warp Rattler. The Jumpers hop up from behind mountains. However, after the Open Space stage of the game, when multiple attacks commence, patterns are of no value. A Big Core Fighter always appears after the Volcanic Stage.

Beginner's Strategy: The game commences with waves of

Fans followed by Rugurrs and other lesser ships. Your principal objective should be to destroy *all* of the Fans and gather Power Capsules. Do this by leaving the control button *alone!* Don't budge, don't slow, don't speed up, don't move up or down . . . just go *straight ahead,* shooting, and everything you need will come to you. By the time you face the first Dakker (on the top of the screen, crawling upside down on some rocks), you should have armed yourself with a laser (first), missiles (second), and double projectiles (third). (Note: only the diagonal projectiles will fire. The laser cannon cannot be used with the nose cannon.)

Now you must start moving around, since the enemy will begin firing at you. The key to avoiding alien fire is to stay away from the far left side of the screen. If they pin you against the edge and send a diagonal barrage your way, they're going to sweep you into the corner and end your not-so-illustrious career. When you reach the mountains that have tunnels bored through them, go *over* the peaks. Ignore them. Though they tempt you with a lot of points and Power Capsules, it's a sucker's move, a poison apple. More often than not, as soon as you're inside, Bacterion ships descend on the mountain. You have no mobility up and down and no way to escape once they start firing at you. If your ship is destroyed, you lose your power boosts—and, thus, will be unable to get through the Volcanic Stage. (If you *do* decide to dare these tunnels, and a mass of ships attack, depress the left side of the control button, slowing down as the ships descend. This will give you a little more time to vaporize them.) While you're in this final portion of the Open Space stage, make a point of collecting enough Power Capsules to get the "ghost ship." That, and the laser cannon, are the principal tools you'll need to blast the volcanic rocks.

When you have them, *don't* go into the volcano field. Stay in the lower left-hand corner of the screen, your cannon level with the top of the nearest volcano. As soon as the rocks begin spitting out, just hover in place and blast them as they emerge from the crater. Don't try to get through the volcanoes using just a force field. That's certain oblivion. You'll face a Big Core Fighter next, which is easy to defeat if you stay on the far-left side of the screen and fire into its heart.

Advanced Strategy: The shield is virtually indispensable if you're going to survive the Stonehenge Stage. Once you've become proficient at dodging the Bacterion ships and their projectiles, position your Warp Rattler on the *right-* hand side of the screen. You'll have less time to react, since the Bacterion vessels are coming from the right. However, this gives you plenty of room to back up and either dodge projectiles or shoot Dakkers, Dai #01, or any other enemy arms you want to attack. Two clues for advanced battles: when the tentacled monsters come at you, keep shooting at their orange heads. And when you finally meet the evil brain, don't be intimidated by the purely decorative bolts of electricity. Stay on the left, midway up the screen, and keep firing. The brain dies easy! There is also an option that only true pros deserve to know, one of which allows you to begin the game with missiles, two ghost ships, and a force field. To access this, begin the game, and as soon as your ship appears, push Start (pause). Then move the controller up, up, down, down, to the left, to the right, left again, right again, then press button B, button A, and deactivate pause. You'll be armed to the teeth and ready to kick some Bacside.

Par: A good player will be scoring 30,000 points in Open Space within an hour. A total of 90,000 points after completing the Stonehenge Stage is good, and an overall tally of 250,000 for one complete eight-round game is average.

NES Advantage: The Slow mode helps a great deal, especially when you have to negotiate through a mass of enemy vehicles, need to pick your way through the Stonehenge level, and so forth. Turbo gives you a faster spray of cannon fire. In fact, using the Advantage, you don't have to do a thing to get through the Open Space phase of the game! Just hold down the trigger button and the controller does the rest.

Training Tips: This is a game that should *not* be played with the thumb working the buttons. Hold the controller as you would a flat camera, with your middle finger on button A (the trigger) and your index finger on button B (the "power booster"). You must be able to hit button B quickly to add the missiles, laser, etc., to your arsenal—but you can't afford to take your finger off the trigger to do it.

Rating: It'll be a warm day on Pluto before you've completely mastered the intricacies of *Gradius*. Though it isn't much of an improvement visually over old video games like *Defender* and *Zaxxon*, you'll be too busy ducking and accelerating to notice. The music is slightly more atmospheric than in most games.

Challenge: A+
Graphics: B
Sound Effects: C+

CHAPTER THIRTEEN

IKARI WARRIORS

Type: Military search-and-destroy.

Objective: Soldiers Paul and Vince (Rambo?) fly into enslaved Ikari with orders to invade, kill, and ultimately, destroy the enemy leader and free the country.

Layout: The heroes begin their battle in the jungles, moving to lakes, bridges, and past smaller fortresses to the steel and brick enemy stronghold. There, they must scurry along pipes to defeat the despot in-the-flesh.

Scroll: The view is from above as the heroes move vertically, from the bottom of the screen to the top.

Hero's Powers: The basic warrior comes equipped with a gun and 100 bullets, plus 50 hand grenades. Along the way he can acquire a Tank and a Helicopter, as well as the following material, which is indicated by large symbols or letters lying on the ground: extra bullets (a gun symbol), super-powerful bullets (F), long-range bullets (L), rapid-fire bullets (S), more grenades (grenade symbol), more *powerful* grenades (B), a knife (knife symbol), death to all foes who are on the screen (except for submerged soldiers) (K), energy for the Tanks or the hero (a gas-tank symbol), super-fuel that lasts longer (H), super-speed walking ability (SS), buck-shot that fires in 3 different directions at once (a 3-pellet symbol), and Hearts, which allow you to retain your munitions even if you die (heart symbol). (Note: The Heart does not work if your third fighter dies and you choose to resume the game.) In phase one of the war (which lasts through the

7-gate fortress), you will only encounter the grenades, bullets, fuel can, knife, and F, L, S, K, B. Many of these items will be found by killing Red Soldiers or destroying Tochikas —the installations with the skull on top. Green Soldiers have only one power to offer, but it's a good one: they're a veritable K mart.

Hero's Weaknesses: Our heroes can be slain by bullets, grenades, Tanks, cannon, Mines, Sensors, flamethrowers, soldiers, and insects (see About Your Enemies).

About Your Enemies: The most important thing to know is that you've got a *ton* of adversaries. (See Beginner's Strategy and Advanced Strategy for specifics.)

Menu: There are two versions: one player controls 3 soldiers, or two players control one soldier each, simultaneously. If one player's soldier dies, another will replace it . . . as long as the other soldier is still alive. The layout is the same for each version.

Timer: None. The only thing that'll stop the game is if your bare-chested juggernauts die or run out of ammunition.

Scoring: Depending upon which soldiers you kill, you earn from 100 to 1000 points (the big sums are for Macho Man, Task Force Soldiers, and Oil Drum Soldiers). Insects net you 200 points, while Fortresses, Gates, Walls, and Tanks earn from 200 to 1000. Each time you pick up armaments of any kind, you earn 200 points. There are also little-known objects that give you moderate to huge sums: a Golden Heart earns you 200, a Radio gets 1000, a Watch is 2000, the dancing girl Little Athena nets 2500, and the Silver and Gold bars each get you 5000 points.

Patterns: The terrain and location of Soldiers, power sources, strongholds, Gates, etc., are always the same.

Beginner's Strategy: It's a cinch to mow down Blue Soldiers, Bazooka Soldiers, Red Soldiers, Diving Soldiers, Green Soldiers, Flamethrower Soldiers, Explosive Soldiers, and Guided Bazooka Soldiers. All of them will fall before bullets, grenades, and/or the Tank (in the Tank, shooting them *or* running them down will do the trick). Note: Since Flamethrower Soldiers can only shoot ahead, approach them from the side. Tougher to deal with are the club-swinging Macho Men and Oil Drum Soldier (one grenade will kill them), the Insects (one grenade each . . . though they move quickly and are less than anxious to go to bug heaven), the shield-carrying Task Force Soldiers (two grenades are required), vehicles, Rock Faces (stone citadels that spit arrows at you), Gates, Walls (one grenade apiece), and Heavy Tanks (two grenades). Helicopters look intimidating, firing salvos of 3 shells each, but they are vulnerable to a single grenade. Each shell from your own Tank packs roughly the same wallop as a grenade. Mines (boxes with an X in the middle) and Sensors (squares with a red orb) are indestructible. The only effective tactic is to run from them.

As you begin your trek, watch for the following landmarks: the small Tochika immediately to the left will provide you with grenades. When you reach the enemy Tank to the right of the 3 rocks, destroy it for 2 cans of fuel. The Tochika before the first vertical bridge conceals a gun; the vehicle after the bridge has more bullets and grenades. The first Gate will provide you with grenades and more bullets, and the Tank just beyond it contains 2 cans of fuel. Note: When you reach a Gate, there will be Snipers on the walls. To defeat them, line yourself up with each one and treat them, in turn, to one of your grenades. Only when they're dead should you blow up the Gate. Make your own map of what other supplies can be found where. Keep in mind, though, that if your own Tank is running low on fuel, and you come upon another, you can switch Tanks. If you're well-fueled, use artillery to *destroy* your extra Tank: Enemies in the immediate vicinity will be torn to pieces.

In the first phase of play the only real problem areas come after you cross the lake. There's a Gate guarded by a pair of Rock Faces. They're situated on opposite sides in such a way that if you run through, there's no avoiding their arrows. Walk past the first Rock Face (located on the left) and stop between the flow of arrows. Wait until there's a gap in the stream of arrows from the head on the right before darting ahead. When you reach the final fortress with its multitude of Gates, make sure you're packing as many grenades as possible. The Gates are staggered as you move to each succeeding wall—located to the left, to the right, and so on—and there are Snipers guarding all of them (there are 7 on the last wall alone). You'll have to stop and kill them all before you can get through.

Special strategy for a two-player game: If you come across one of your own Tanks, put *both* Paul and Vince in the machine, simultaneously hit the A button on each controller, and each man will have a Tank! Also, if you're in a Tank that is about to explode (it turns a sickly gray), you don't necessarily have to die with it. Simply press down the A and B buttons simultaneously and you'll survive.

Advanced Strategy: The second phase is more difficult, largely because there are so many more soldiers. Tanks are essential here. Things to watch out for: there are a pair of Snipers on either side of the open field which lies between the 4 bombed-out buildings and the Tochika; 2 Helicopters await you after the second of the 2 small vertical bridges; you can get bullets and grenades by destroying the Tochika just beyond the lake; there are 7 Snipers hidden in the 3-Gate complex that lies beyond the second lake; a Knife and Heart can be found in the complex just after the small river; and the first Macho Man is waiting for you right beyond the complex Gate. There are 2 more Macho Men in the field before the long vertical bridge (watch for them after you pass the Tochika nestled to the left of a large rock). As for the hidden treasures, when you go through the first Gate, turn left: There are Bars on the left side of the Wall (the one you just passed through, *not* the Wall in front of you). A Watch can be found smack in the center of the first *narrow* river, and two more are located on the first Wall at the maze of Walls, on the left and right sides; additional Bars are in the pyramid-shaped Rock behind the center of the fourth Wall; Little Athena is doing her belly dance on the right side of the second Wall beyond the Gold; and the Radio is in the second maze of Walls, hidden in the Wall to the right of and just beyond the second Sensor.

If at any time you bite the bullet, you can continue a game at the same stage where you left off (though without whatever supplies you've gathered) simply by pushing A, B, B, A on the controller before "Game Over" flashes on the screen. There's also another trick, although you have to be the Flash to make it work: plug in the game cartridge, and while the two soldiers are firing *(before* the menu appears) rapidly input the following code using the controller and the A and B buttons: up, down, A, A, B, left, right, A, B, up, A, down, right, right, left, B, up, left, A, right, B, left, right, A, left, up, A, down, A, right, left, B, Select. That will allow you to access any stage you wish . . . provided you can punch in the entire sequence in *5 seconds!* When all is said and done, however, the best strategy of all is to become Fort Bragg with legs: arm yourself with everything you can and forge ahead!

Par: You should have 12,000 points by the time you reach the first horizontal bridge, and 45,000 points when you come upon the Helicopter. After crossing the second vertical bridge, you should have a score of at least 75,000. At the end of phase one, 100,000 is average. A Stallone Jr. should be able to rack up a quarter of a million points in a game.

NES Advantage: No help here.

Training Tips: Ignore scoring points for a few rounds. Get into a tank, and later, a Helicopter, and stay out of jeopardy so that you can map Ikari.

Rating: The game's a real odyssey, and there are always plenty of things to shoot. Unfortunately, the graphics leave a lot to be desired, and precision shooting is often difficult because of that.

Challenge: B+
Graphics: D
Sound Effects: C

CHAPTER FOURTEEN

KARNOV

Type: Fantasy search-and-destroy.

Objective: When the foul Dragon Ryu steals the Treasure of Babylon from the small town of Creamina, the hearty Russian hero Jinborov Karnovski (a.k.a. Karnov, a former circus strongman) agrees to go and get it. But before he can face Ryu and recover the Treasure, he must cross 9 deadly lands and face an army of vile foes.

Layout: On-screen are the various realms through which Karnov must pass.

Scroll: The picture moves from side to side, for the most part, though when Karnov ascends a peak or dives underwater, it moves up and down. Note: In *most* cases, once the screen has moved behind Karnov, he can't return to it. There are a few exceptions, however, as when he travels underwater.

Hero's Powers: At the onset of his argosy, Karnov has the power to shoot fireballs, to jump, and to crouch. (Be warned, though, shooting while he walks slows him down.) He also has 3 lives and the ability to take 2 hits before he dies. (He turns sickly gray after the first hit, though his abilities are undiminished.) As he moves along, he can collect double- and triple-fireball power by picking up red orbs; an orb will also restore Karnov's natural hue if he's taken a hit and is in his gray stage. (If it does this, however, it will not boost him to the next fireball level.)

There are many other power Options Karnov can add to his arsenal, indicated by symbols in small boxes that lie around the terrain, hang in the air or underwater, etc. These are Jumping Boots, which double Karnov's leaping ability; Bombs, for limited-range destruction; Ladders, for climbing; K's, 50 of which will give Karnov an extra life (you can't store these: at 50, the life is automatically granted and you must begin collecting anew); Boomerangs, which are powerful but must be caught when they return or are forfeited; Clappers, to clear the screen of enemies (except the titans at the end of each level); Glasses, which permit him to see concealed Options; Wings for flight; a Swimming Mask, which increases Karnov's speed underwater; and a Shield, which gives Karnov added invulnerability. Jumping Boots and Wings last for approximately 15 seconds each. Most of these powers can be stockpiled; many players also don't realize that one Ladder can be stored for later use by climbing down, rather than by taking the easy way and leaping down. Note: Your collected powers are displayed at the bottom of the screen and are accessed by hitting Start, moving the controller until the Option you want is flashing, then pressing Select. However, many powers are not accessible until the *computer* causes them to flash. Fortunately, this happens at the right time; for example, the Wings can be used when you face the Snake Woman.

Hero's Weaknesses: Being hit by monsters or their projectiles, or running out of time, will terminate a life.

About Your Enemies: The big terrors await Karnov at the end of each land. Among them: the Fish Monster, which shoots projectiles and leaps up and down; the Lion Keeper, who tosses knives if you have the good fortune to kill its bullet-spitting Lion; the Tyrannosaurus, which breathes fireballs; the Snake Woman, who also exhales death as she slithers toward you, and who gets stronger with every passing moment; another Tyrannosaurus, which is even tougher than the first; Gidora, a two-headed winged serpent that belches twin fireballs; and Ryu, which is roughest of all. Among the lesser (but no less deadly) monsters are Chicken Bones, vultures that wait in trees and spit fire; Rock Men, who toss boulders at the hero; Stone Men, who shoot bullets; Bounders, acrobats that cluster and pounce on Karnov; Bats; Killer Clams; Volcanoes; the Golden Knight, who splits into a spray of deadly balls; the Invisible Knights, who toss daggers as they approach from both sides; spear-tossing Merpeople; Air Serpents that come when you reuse your Ladder; Sea Serpents; Piranhas; Floaters, green ogres that drift toward you; Biters, which come from the sky in swarms; Killer Balls, which zip through the skies; and Pteranodons. (Note: Not all of these names are "officially sanctioned." However, neither the instructions nor the game provide a dramatis personae.)

Menu: There is only the one-player odyssey.

Timer: You have 250 seconds (the timer functions in real-time) to clear each level.

Scoring: Karnov collects points as he travels. Most monsters earn from 30 to 100 points; the end-of-level varmints start at 300, Options get you 50, and glowing red orbs are 100. The total is displayed as the hero finishes a level.

Patterns: The location of the monsters and the landscape are almost always the same. (Exceptions are rare. For example, on rare occasion Biters will attack when you land on the ledge of the Killer Balls in level three. Bounders usually pounce before you climb the peak that leads to the Volcanoes; now and then, they stay away.) Options are always found in the same places. Occasionally, though, some Options will pop up as a bonus. For instance, at the end of the first level Wings will sometimes show up on the face of the building before you must battle the Fish Monster; now and then a Ladder can be found at the bottom of the sea. However, these are merely icing on the cake. The Options you will rely on, and need, are always in the same place.

Beginner's Strategy: First and foremost, *Karnov* is won by getting as many Options as possible. Don't pass up anything, if you don't have to. To begin, hop onto the pillars, get the glowing red ball, hop down to get the Ladder, go down and back to the columns, extend the Ladder and get the Jumping Boots. Collect the K next, then go down and to the right . . . jumping up and shooting the Rock Man while leaping the boulder he threw. (You can also kill him by standing on the last column, jumping to the one on the left to bring him into view, then jumping back onto the last column and shooting down. This is actually safer, since the rocks can't touch you here.) Get the Bomb, continue onward—crouching and spinning from side to side as soon as the first puffs of smoke appear (indicating the arrival of Chicken Bone's soldiers). Take them out, then hop up and blast Chicken Bone itself. It won't start shooting at you until it descends. Grab the glowing red ball behind its tree. You now have triple-fireball power and should breeze through this level. Collect the K's that lie ahead . . . staying at midscreen and shooting the monsters that approach. Make sure you stop short of the water. If you fall in, you'll perish. Backtrack when you have all the K's, then climb the stairs. When you reach the end of the cityscape (there's a desert beyond), raise your Ladder and get the Boomerang, which is out of view, to the right of the last building. Move ahead cautiously. As soon as the Fish Monster materializes, crouch and shoot your fireballs. When the amphibian leaps, slide over to the right, spin, shoot, and send it to an early grave.

You'll be transported now to the second level. Here you'll immediately face 3 stone heads that spit bullets. Watch the right: as soon as the first one shows its profile, jump up and blast it. If the bullets come down at you, crouch to avoid them. It takes 3 shots to disintegrate the stone. Hurry to the column on which it was resting. Leap up and shoot the second head, ducking behind the column for protection. When the second statue is destroyed, jump up to the far right side of the first column. Hop up, blasting the third head and ducking as necessary. Ascend to the third column, jump to the ledge and get the Wings, turn quickly and jump back to the column to avoid the Rock Man's boulder (it will fall harmlessly to the ground). Move ahead. When you reach the ledge, don't leap into the pit, simply *slide* down the steps. (A jump would carry you into a fireball shot from the stone head on the right.) When you reach the bottom, a Golden Knight will appear on the right; crouch and start shooting when you get halfway across. The creature will die before it can split. *Hurry* up the stairs, shooting the Bounders. The longer it takes you to get to and up the steps, the more Bounders there will be. Ascend quickly, crossing the ledge while you leap fireballs from the stone face on the left (if you get to the ledge fast, you can take the flamers in one jump, leaping up and left). Hurry to the right and wait by the electrified fence: Monster birds will arrive in 2 rows. Shooting rapidly to the left, you'll clip their wings before they can break rank and attack you. Next up, atop the staircase, is a monster canine. Wait on the last step; hop up, shoot it, and duck down, using the step as protection until the creature is dead. Moving to the right, you will face the knife-throwing Invisibles. Again, as soon as they *begin* to materialize, crouch and fire from side to side. Continue on, picking up the extra pair of Boots. The Lion Tamer and his chained feline will arrive, then: crouch and shoot as soon as they show their sneering kissers. If you still have triple-fireball power, they will die before they reach you. If not, put on your Jumping Boots and try to get behind them when they approach, so you can continue shooting. There is no passing to another level simply by going to the right; you've got to score against these professors of evil to be promoted.

The third level begins with a Chicken Bone. Kill it by jumping up before it can fly down and start exhaling projectiles. Once you are past it, grab the red ball and climb the tree. At the top, face right and simultaneously press the jump button and push the controller to the right. You'll land on a ledge. Fire as you drop, in case Biters arrive. If not, move ahead and stand still as the Deadly Balls begin to form. Wait to see which way this string of killer-spheres moves, then move in that direction. They will double back at you; when they do, blast away, continuing to shoot until the last one disintegrates. Use your Ladder to climb and get the Jumping Boots, then go back to the left edge of the cliff to Ladder-up and get both the glowing orb and the Swimming Mask. Biters will arrive as you set up your Ladder; keep shooting to the right. An Air Serpent will certainly show up now. Blast it behind the head; 4 hits will do the trick (it glows when struck). You *must* get rid of this monster, or it will keep chasing you. Climb down, and use short hops to clear the small pits. Enter the last jump shooting, since there will be Stone Men and other vermin waiting on the other side. At this point you will also have a chance to drop into a pit and pick up a fortune in K's. Do it: Above, you will have to face Fish Monsters, among other nettlesome beasts. As soon as you land on the bottom, start shooting; a Golden Knight will soon appear. Gather the K's, enter the last part of the tunnel firing in case another Knight appears, climb, and continue. You'll face several Rock Men and other menaces on a series of steps, which can be dealt with using a hop-shoot-hop routine. Above the edge of the last cliff, there will be a Shield; get it, use it, jump down, and face Mr. Rex. You can't jump over him very well, so it will be necessary to start hitting him as soon as he shows. All it takes to make him extinct are 3 shots to the head, requiring a total of 3 leaps with triple-fireball power. And you, my friend, are off to the ice world. Note: Bombs are plentiful, but they're weak and a waste of time. Better to shoot foes rather than waste time by pausing and accessing your inventory.

Advanced Strategy: The fourth level is actually easier than the second or third, largely because powerful weapons are here and they're plentiful. (Surprisingly, for an ice world, the footing is just fine.) Enter shooting the Biters, which will roll down the cliff on the right. Hop up and kill the first Chicken Bone, climb, then bound up to shoot the second Bone as soon as it appears. When you reach the Glasses, get them and climb up one more step. Go to the extreme right of that step so the Rock Man will appear above and to the right. Immediately raise your Ladder, climb to the Clapper, and, while you're on the Ladder—above Rock Man's rolling stones—plug him. Press on. When you reach the Rock Man on a flat rock (it's the one slightly higher than the rock to the left of it), stand on that left-side rock and shoot him. You won't be hurt. As soon as he dies, rush across the plain in great leaps, and when you reach the mountain, climb. Bounders will show up on the plain, but if you're quick, they won't bother you. Kill the Rock Man on top using hop-shoot-hop, then climb down the other side. Wait for the volcanic craters to spew; as soon as they both fall silent, race over them. The tunnels here are easy to negotiate by shooting and running. When you find the Wings, seize them. (Note: After you face the Bounders, you'll have a chance to go down a ladder and gather K's. Don't take it unless you already have Wings. Even then, an extra pair wouldn't hurt. If you go down, you'll return to the surface on the ledge with the Snake Woman. That won't give you much time to prepare to fight her.) At the edge of the vast pit take flight, head to the top center of the screen, and start blasting away to the right. When the Snake Woman drops from above, you'll be hitting her square in the face. Descend with her, shooting triple fireballs all the while. By the time she reaches the ledge she'll be dead.

You'll find yourself at the Sea World now. Leap off the cliff and don your Swimming Mask as soon as it flashes. You'll face 2 waves of Piranhas, after which a Sea Serpent will attack from the left. Swim *toward* it. When it's ahead of you, shoot it behind the head. When it dies, another may come immediately, so be alert! Blast the bullet-spitting weeds on the ledge, descend and gather K's (shooting the Monster Clam), and watch out for the Merpeople. Their spears not only travel horizontally, but vertically. Since there are Clappers underwater, don't hesitate to use any you have stockpiled to kill the Merpeople. You can swim under the land masses and/or cross them; do both. You'll gather K's below, and armaments above.

When you face the next Tyrannosaurus, you can do several things; the best is either to whip out a Boomerang (one hit in the head will kill it), or use the Ladder to get above it, chucking fireballs to destroy it. (Note, by the way, that on this and future levels, you can be done-in for want of a Ladder or Jumping Boots; there are many objects in the sky which only they can get to. Karnov is spirited next to a field where he is set upon by knife-tossing Knights. Duck and use your spin-and-shoot technique. Monsters will float at you; jump their bullets while you shoot them, then climb the building (take a huge jump to get onto the first ladder; it will get you away from the clustering monsters). Fish Men will attack from the right; climb fast to avoid their projectiles, simultaneously shooting at them. Get the Crystal on the other side of the skyscraper. Every *other* Chicken Bone roosting here will attack you, after which you'll face another Snake Woman. Grab the Shield you'll find, and shoot her. She's much easier to slay than her predecessor.

The next site opens with 3 more stone heads . . . and a passel of Bounders. Shoot the latter as you go forward, and kill the statues as before. Climb the Pyramid and drop down the pit bordered by the two Clappers. (You *could* have gone straight at the base of the Pyramid, but then you wouldn't have gotten this weapon.) Go all the way to the bottom and kill the Mummy there (rapid shots accompanied by leaping the projectiles it throws). Get the Crystal and climb until you reach the room of the Golden Door. Use your Ladder to reach it, and enter. That will cause a stone path and a Mummy to appear. Leap the Mummy and jump down, fold up your Ladder, move it to the left, climb and crouch on the top, and kill the Mummy. Go to the last stone on the left; the floor will give way beneath you. In short order you'll reach Gidora, the two-headed winged serpent. Stand as far to the right as you can, and, with a Shield for protection, begin shooting at the monster's heads. Back up as you fire; it will perish before you do.

You will now be whisked to the next-to-last level. Wings will appear above you; get them, then fly to the base of the bullet-spitting statue. Get the Shield and a second pair of Wings there, fly up, and, with the Shield, block the statue's bullets while shooting at its eye. This will kill it. Fly up, get the Crystal, and then fly through the passage over the statue's head. Your Wings will run out by now, and donning another pair, shoot the second statue in the eye. (You *can* squeeze through the passage over it's head while it's shooting . . . but touching the statue will turn you blue.) Right past the second head you'll see a Crystal in a wall. Alight on the left side of the wall and use bombs to blow it down. (It'll take 3 explosions to get through.) Get the Wings there, fly past the Chicken Bones, and leap from pillar to pillar when your Wings expire. When you come to a precipice, make a leap-of-faith: There's a ledge off-screen, and you'll land on it. (Obviously, if you still have Wings, use 'em!) Kill the Gidora here as you did the last one, and, voilà! You'll find yourself at the incredible ninth level, where you will face virtually every lesser monster you battled on previous levels.

Upon arriving, use the Ladder to collect all the goodies overhead. As it turns out, in this level all roads lead to Ryu; whichever way you walk, you'll reach a wall that will magically vanish and let you into a room with 3 windows and a stone dragon's head. Ryu's own three heads will emerge from the windows and, using all your weapons, you'll be in for the fight of your life! Make sure you jump up, so you're over the windows, when you battle the vicious serpent.

Par: You should be able to finish each level with an *average* of 30,000 points (earlier levels will be less, circa 8000 points; later levels more).

NES Advantage: With the regular controller it's a pain to keep pressing the button to fire. Holding down the Advantage button allows you to spew continuous death.

Training Tips: Most of the skills you'll need can be polished on the first level. Stay here, shooting, crouching, jumping—and, most important, learning to hit the Select button without looking down, so you can pause the action to access your Options. On the other hand, if you're restless for some *real* action, you can hop ahead to any level you wish as follows. Wait until the title screen comes on. When it does, on controller one, hold down—at the same time—the A and B buttons, the Select button, and simultaneously push the controller to the right. While you're doing this use the A button on the second controller to advance to the stage you want. (You'll have to count, since nothing but the title will be displayed on the screen. To make things even more confusing, you'll have to press the A button one *less* time than the level you want. For example, if you want to start on level 8, press the button 7 times.) When you've reached the level you want, push Start on controller one. You'll automatically begin on the level you wish.

Rating: After maybe a dozen times you'll get the hang of what you need to fight whom, and the hop-shoot-hop rhythm will be second nature. After that it's fun to try and beat your time, and also to find new ways of killing the monsters (for example, using the Boomerang instead of triple fireballs).

Challenge: B
Graphics: B
Sound Effects: B—

CHAPTER FIFTEEN

KID ICARUS

Type: Fantasy quest.

Objective: As the youthful angel, Kid Icarus (also known as Pit), you're a tad overwhelmed by the task you're given: Sent from Angel Land, you must pass through the Underworld, the Overworld, and the Skyworld, to reach the Palace in the Sky. There, you must duke it out with the nefarious Medusa and rescue the precious Princess of Light, Palutena.

Layout: The hero enters a series of rooms and can move in any direction. Each world has four distinct "areas" through which the hero must venture.

Scroll: The screen moves from side to side or up and down, depending upon which way Icarus travels.

Hero's Powers: When he sets out, poor Icarus can do nothing more than jump, duck, come to sudden stops, and shoot arrows. As he forges ahead he can win Angel Feathers to break his falls; Holly Bows to boost the power of his arrows; Light Arrows, which are extremely potent; a Crystal, which preserves him from harm; the Water of Life, which replenishes Icarus' strength; the Water Barrel for storing extra Water; a Mirror Shield, for defense; Fire, which enlarges the Kid's arrows; a Big Hammer, which packs far more wallop than an arrow; a Harp, to transform his foes into those very useful Big Hammers; Pegasus' Wings, for flight; a Credit Card for charging things in shops (obtained by triumphing against every foe and target in the Treasure

Room); and a Check Sheet, Torch, and Pencil, which enable him to see exactly where he is in any area. Goods can be purchased; many can also be found in the special rooms that dot the landscape (see Beginner's Strategies, below).

Hero's Weaknesses: If Icarus is blasted or pounced upon by monsters (see About Your Enemies), falls from a ledge, or tumbles into any trap, the Princess is going to grow old in captivity.

About Your Enemies: *Kid Icarus* is a veritable museum of monsters. There are over *forty* in all, among them: the tentacled orb Monoeye; the snaking Kobil; the flaming McGoo; the Pac-Man-like Minos; the beaked Nettler; Girin, which spits bullets from its mouth; Specknose (believe it or not, he looks like those funny glasses with a false nose and moustache); Mick, a pair of ravaging teeth; Snowman, who flings iceballs at Icarus; the Eggplant Wizard, who transforms you into the vaunted food staple; the Reaper and Reapettes, whose touch is death; Keron, a flying toad; Rokman, who pounds the hero with his stony body; Tamambo, a biting brass ball; Hewdraw, a huge serpent; and the lumbering quadruped Twinbellows.

Menu: There is only the one great adventure.

Timer: None.

Scoring: You get points for making your way through the worlds. Also, as you travel you will be gathering Currency Units, which you need to buy things. These appear whenever Icarus is victorious against an adversary; the monster transforms into a Heart. (You might say the baddies have a *change* of heart. . . .) A Small Heart gives him one unit, a Half-Heart 5, and a Big Heart 10.

Patterns: The rooms, shops, and appearance of the monsters are always the same.

Beginner's Strategy: The most important aspect of any quest game is knowing the terrain *and* how to negotiate it. In this case, the Underworld begins with ledges haunted by the serpentine Kobils. On the fourth level up you'll find God's Room. Fill your quiver, then continue up the ledges. On the second of the staircases that leads to the left, beware of Monoeyes. Let them near, then shoot them. Mount the thin steps carefully, then climb the seven gray stone ledges. A Treasure Room awaits on the platform above. When you reach the second area of the Underworld, proceed with caution; the ledges are covered with ice. Be ready to press the controller in the direction *opposite* that of your skid, or else dig in your heels by tapping the controller up.

Along the way keep notes about what treasures are hidden where, and in what sequence. For example, in the Treasure Room of the first area of the Underworld, go to the upper left and get the goods in that Pitcher first. Descend and get the treasure below it next. If both of these are Hearts, retrieve what's in the Pitcher in the lower right. If it's a Hammer, go to the bottom left and get the treasure there, then move to the middle ledge on the right and gather the goods there. Save the top right ledge last. *However:* If there's a Heart in the lower right, get the treasure on the top right and middle right (in that order) before heading to the Pitcher in the lower left. If the upper and middle left ledges both contain Hammers, go next to the treasure on the ledge in the middle; if they were a Hammer and Heart, respectively, hie thee to the middle ledge on the right. As for the Shops, it's always useful to try and bargain with merchants. This can be done by tapping the A and B button of the second controller *concurrently*. More often than not the merchant will come back with lower prices for goods. (Alas, one in five times haggling will only make him grumpier and he'll *raise* the price.)

Make sure you know how to get to the Hot Spring Room to nurse your wounds before meeting Twinbellows at the end of the Underworld. When you enter the fourth area, head left 2 rooms, down 2 rooms, then left one room. Also, note how to reach the Hospital in case you've been transformed into an Eggplant. Upon reaching the fourth area, go right 3 rooms, then up one. There's another Hot Spring Room a short distance into the Overworld, and another not far beyond it, in area two.

Advanced Strategy: If you've mastered the ins and outs of moving through the early areas, the latter realms are difficult largely because of the monsters you'll encounter. Some

79

important strategies are as follows. Lesser demons are easily beaten: the Reaper, for instance, by shooting it in the back (this is no time for fair play!), the Snowman by shooting from below, and the Eggplant Wizard by firing between the flurries of eggplants. Destroying the evil Bosses of each world is somewhat more difficult. When you tackle Twinbellows in the last room of the Underworld, secret yourself in back of a column (thus protecting you from projectiles) and, as the beast approaches, hit it with rapid-fire bursts. Hurry to the other side and repeat. When you face Hewdraw at the end of the Overworld, continuously leap over the leviathan and shoot at its head. As for Medusa, you can't battle the head Boss unless you've obtained the Light Arrow, Mirror Shield, and Pegasus' Wings. When you reach your nemesis, your best approach is to go to the top left side of the screen and come right a few taps (just under one third the length of the screen). Keep facing to the right so Medusa's beams can't hurt you. When the Snake slithers by, drop down so you can shoot Medusa's pupil, skewer it, then continue to descend. When the Snake goes by, rise, blast the monster's pupil again, and continue to ascend. Continue this pattern over and over until the creature is "stone dead."

Par: 25,000 is a good point tally for each area of every world.

NES Advantage: The joystick makes it a great deal easier to move Icarus with precision.

Training Tips: Practice your jumping, especially the jump followed by a crouch. Unless this is second nature to you, you won't be able to move and duck and also fire when it comes time to battle your adversaries.

Rating: Although *Kid Icarus* doesn't have quite the same sense of wonder as *Solomon's Key*, or the exotic look of *Mega Man*, it is innovative in its various pitfalls (the ice is great), sense of humor, and in the hero's powers.

Challenge: A—
Graphics: B
Sound Effects: B

CHAPTER SIXTEEN

KID-NIKI

Type: Fantasy search-and-destroy.

Objective: You are Kid-Niki, the "Radical Ninja," and your beloved Princess Margo has been abducted by the *un*-beloved Stone Wizard. You hasten to rescue her, undaunted by the many monsters that lie in wait.

Layout: The screen shows each of the 7 realms Niki must cross to save his girlfriend.

Scroll: The hero moves from left to right, with limited mobility from top to bottom.

Hero's Powers: The Kid begins with 3 lives and a Spinning Sword, which he whirls like a billyclub to kill anyone who comes near. As he proceeds, he slays creatures or enters hidden rooms to gain weapons and/or points. The arms are a Golden Bell, whose chime slays from a distance; a Silver Bell, which creates an impenetrable shield of sound around Niki; a Mini-Niki, which bestows an extra life; and a Mini-Princess, which averts one death. These weapons (except for the final 2) last for an average of 15 seconds.

Hero's Weaknesses: Getting touched by a monster or anything it emits (which may include something as innocuous-looking as Bubbles), falling off a ledge or cliff, or running out of time, will kill Niki.

About Your Enemies: The rottenest foes are the Big Bosses Niki must fight at the end of each land. These are: Death Breath; Spike, the Stone Buddha; the Horned Witch; the Green Grub; the Mad Monk; the Samurai Guard; and the

Stone Wizard himself. Numerous lesser monsters inhabit each land. Each of these is a small bounding or flying creature. Be aware that *everything* that moves is an enemy—including sweet-looking birdies. (See Beginner's Strategy and Advanced Strategy for details on several creatures.)

Menu: There is only the one game.

Timer: Niki has 6 minutes to cross each land (the clock moves in real time).

Scoring: Niki earns points for each creature he slays, as well as bonus points for Coins he collects and for the amount of time that remains on the clock when he finishes each land.

Patterns: The realms, as well as the approach and location of the monsters therein, are always the same.

Beginner's Strategy: In general, whenever you kill a Big Boss, make sure you jump up and grab the Scroll they leave behind; you will be rewarded. There's nothing to give you much trouble on the first level. Kill the stationary birds with a high jump-knife combination and dispatch other foes with easy blows. When you reach the platform of land at approximately the 5:05 mark, stand at the edge and hit the B button; you'll be spirited to a secret chamber with its hidden goods. When you confront Death Breath, stay on the left, leap when he does, and stab him under his bloated cheek. He will die after 5 such hits. (Note: You will lose your sword with each strike against him and other Big Bosses. Run over and grab it *quickly.)*

On the second level, if you kill every one of the Blue Birds that attacks, you will get a weapon. Climb the first tree you encounter after the clearing (the sixth tree on this level): There's another secret chamber there. When you face Spike, leap over him and let him move to the left. When he reaches either side, he stops swinging his mace for just a moment; that's when you move in and stab him. After the first wound Spike will move back to the right, swinging again; leap him, stab him when he reaches the right side, and repeat. He will die after 5 stabs.

On level three don't be afraid of the precipice you encounter: You can walk on the Clouds. Make sure that you jump on the moving Cloud when it's *down;* it'll carry you past the bird, which, otherwise, you'd have hit. Upon reaching the bridge, touch the Balloon, it'll give you a weapon. The Horned Witch is a unique foe, in that she divides into two smaller Witches each time she's hit (ditto each of the smaller Witches). There's nothing you can do here but to keep on stabbing her diminutive clones.

On the fourth level, wait while the Frogs uncoil their death tongues; attack the instant they're withdrawn. Avoid the Bubbles over the water and jump toward the moving Rock when it's submerged. It'll rise by the time you get there. If you jump when it's raised, it'll go under before you can vacate. When you face the Grub, it'll take at least 8 hits to kill it: Strike its green midsection and head as it passes. Whenever it burrows underground, wait there, your blade spinning, so you'll smack it as soon as it emerges. Don't bother with the tail.

Advanced Strategy: The course becomes considerably more dangerous when you reach the fifth level. As you drop into the fog bank you'll have to establish a jump-and-kick rhythm to defeat the dive-bombing Birds. You must strike each one on your way *up* in a jump, otherwise one of the oncoming Birds is almost certain to kill you. You *can* try jumping them all, though this is extremely difficult due to the fog and the sheer numbers of birds behind and in front of you. When you reach the Buddha, stand in its lap and *wait* for the Bee to attack; if you descend, you'll not only have to deal with it buzzing around, but with the Chubbies as well. When you reach the Monk you'll find him the easiest to slay of all the Big Bosses. Rush to the left base of the pedestal. Stand there, and the Monk will leap off, to the right. Hop onto the platform and kick him in the head, then bolt back to the base. Repeat this procedure several times and the Monk will be destroyed.

The course of the sixth land is relatively easy for the first half. To begin with, stab all the Red Birds to get a weapon. As you move along, ripping up the Kites is easy enough. The Bouncers are a little trickier: It's a good idea to let them stack, then kill several at once. (If you want to plug them one at a time, that's okay . . . as long as they don't leapfrog onto your head. *Whatever* you do, don't let them push you to the left. If you do, and they hop at you, you won't have room to avoid them.) Survival becomes a bit more difficult when you come to the wall and the Bubble-Blowing Baby Monsters. Stab them if you can . . . or just wait. Their pudgy little fingers can't hold onto the ledges for very long and they regularly slip back down the wall. Without a doubt the Golden Samurai is the most dangerous Big Boss to date. He's easy enough to disarm with a jumping stab, but that won't kill him. What you must do is stay to his immediate left and, when he bends to stab you with his staff, leap up. Come down squarely on the point where his staff and head intersect. (Be careful not to jump too soon or you'll skewer your head on his blade.) Several such hits will be required to kill the armored Boss. Important: If the Samurai forces you to the left, you're doomed. He will charge you before you can recover your sword. If he gets as far over as midscreen, simply disarm him. He'll have to chase his weapon to the right. Use the distraction to grab your sword and run to the right. This will give you more room to maneuver.

On the seventh level you will require all of your jumping and stabbing skills to defeat the Stone Wizard. Suffice to say it would be wise to have a Mini Princess in your arsenal before tackling him.

Par: Players should be able to get an average of 35,000 points for each round.

NES Advantage: This is very useful in crowded screens (such as 5), when creatures such as the Bouncers must be hit rapid fire.

Training Tips: As with so many games, once you master the basic skills, you won't have any problem. Stay on the low levels until jumping and stabbing (alone *and* in tandem) are second nature to you. If you have the Advantage, study the later screens using Slow; being aware of who's coming from where will help you to plan a strategy.

Rating: *Kid-Niki* is a charming and modestly challenging game, with gobs of Oriental atmosphere. The monsters are wonderfully designed and quite innovative.

Challenge: B
Graphics: B+
Sound Effects: B

CHAPTER SEVENTEEN

KUNG FU

Type: Martial arts combat.

Objective: The venomous gang leader Mr. X has kidnapped fair Sylvia and lashed her to a chair deep in his ornate estate. As the bold Thomas, you must go from floor to floor, using your martial arts skills to dispatch Mr. X and his dangerous henchfolk in an effort to free the captive.

Layout: There are five floors to the estate. You ascend by reaching the staircase on the side toward which the screen is scrolling. There are no shortcuts; the only way to reach them is by fighting your way through the villains. After you've freed Sylvia, the game starts again—with the villains appearing at an increasingly faster pace.

Scroll: Right to left on floors 1, 3, and 5; left to right on 2 and 4.

Hero's Powers: Thomas has six abilities: the "foot sweep," a low kick; the punch to the jaw; the kick to the chin; the jump kick; the jump punch; and the hug.

Hero's Weaknesses: A power bar on top of the screen keeps track of Thomas's vitality. A knife drains roughly a quarter of his strength, an encounter with a stick takes just over a third. Lose three Thomases, and Sylvia never sees daylight again.

About the Bad Guys: Vanquished foes simply fall off the screen. The Grippers are easy-to-beat thugs with no special powers; the Knife Throwers fling daggers; and the Stick Fighter wields a club (2 blows send Thomas to oblivion). All

86

of these appear on the first floor. The second floor offers these, as well as Dragon Balls, each of which falls from the ceiling and erupts into a Dragon when it hits the ground; Snake Baskets, which fall and become serpents; and Confetti Balls, which drop and fire shrapnel in all directions. The Tom Tom Brothers also appear on this level, somersaulting midgets who vault onto your head. The Giant makes his debut on the third floor. The fourth floor introduces Poisonous Moths, which fly in through the windows, and the Black Magician, who regenerates lost body parts and throws fireballs. Sometimes the fireballs are duds; sometimes they explode and become Snakes or Dragons. Mr. X only appears on the fifth floor. Grippers appear on each floor, as do Knife Throwers.

Menu: One Player A, one Player B, two Players A, two Players B. The principal difference between the A and B games is that there are more enemies on the screen at most times in the B game.

Timer: You must get Thomas across each floor before the 2000 time units run out—the equivalent of one minute 48.8 seconds—or before his strength runs out.

Scoring: Different types of kicks or punches are scored differently, as are foes. After you complete each floor your remaining time and strength earns you extra points. Note: It's a little-known fact, but Thomas will earn a wealth of additional points with two maneuvers. If he can destroy a Dragon *before* it breathes fire, he will receive 2000 extra points. And if he knocks out his twelfth opponent with a jump kick, he'll reap an additional 5000 points! (But beware: If the twelfth opponent is a Knife Thrower or Tom Tom, they don't count and you're out of luck. Also, you have to have done away with the first 11 enemies using kicks or punches, but *no* foot sweeps.)

Patterns: On the first floor of the estate the Grippers tend to arrive in four groups of three, usually from the left. (Occasionally two will come from the left, one from the right.) The first Knife Thrower is either the thirteenth or fourteenth enemy to appear. Knife Throwers almost always throw their knives high on the first toss. If you don't attack them, they wait an average of 3 seconds between knife throws. If you attack, they can throw as many as one every second. Boomerang Throwers also throw high on their initial attack.

Beginner's Strategy: The key to winning the game is to *keep moving* to the left. Don't stand still and wait for enemies to arrive. When they approach from the right, don't turn to meet them immediately. That wastes time. Keep heading left, waiting until they're close before you turn to fight them. Stick mostly to foot sweeps to dispatch your enemies. You won't get as many points, but they're quick, easy, and effective. Kicks can be used, but only against Grippers. When they are bunched together in a group of three, a jump kick—squarely to the chin of the lead Gripper—will knock them all down. When you tackle the Stick Man, use a foot sweep to take him out. This keeps your head out of range of his club. Don't bother with foot sweeps on the Giant: You're going to need a jump kick to get him. If there are enemies behind you, deal with them first; after you jump kick the Giant, you're going to have to back up to get out of range in case the one blow doesn't finish him. Watch for Mr. X to appear immediately after you've passed the small cornice which looks like a stack of black pancakes on a white field. Defeat Mr. X using a foot sweep, which, again, is the easiest. If you beat him, don't stop! Enemies will continue to attack until you reach Sylvia.

Advanced Strategy: When you engage the Stick Fighter, move Thomas close and hug him. The stick is ineffective at close range. When you hear the sound of the club you'll have a second before he swings again—enough time to slide back and do him in with repeated foot sweeps; *or*, if Thomas has a minimum of half his power, try for high-point jump kicks. Mr. X is most vulnerable to a jump kick. Weaken him with a flurry of foot sweeps, then fell him with a single jumper.

Par: First floor, 700 time units; second floor, 700; third floor, 900; fourth floor, 600; and fifth floor, 900. A good point tally for all five floors is 160,000 points (this is computed using the number of foes you've killed, how you've killed them, and how much energy Thomas has left).

NES Advantage: Use of Slow gives you time to analyze an attack and plan your response. This is best when, for example, you are faced with Knife Throwers coming from opposite sides of the screen. The use of Turbo allows you to pivot rapidly from left to right and to deliver a continuous rain of kicks or punches just by holding down the button. Turbo is of no advantage on the jump maneuvers.

Training Tips: Play with the sound turned off. Nifty as the grunts and shouts are, they can be distracting.

Rating: You'll master this one quickly, though it's fun to let out your frustrations by beating up Mr. X and his unctuous allies.

Challenge: C
Graphics: C
Sound Effects: B+

CHAPTER EIGHTEEN

THE LEGEND
OF KAGE

Type: Martial arts search-and-destroy.

Objective: When the lovely Princess Kiri, daughter of a powerful Shogun, is abducted while strolling through the woods, the Ninja Kage sets out to rescue her.

Layout: Kage slashes his way through 4 terrains: the Forest, the Passage, the Fortress, and the Castle. When he finishes, he starts all over again, though his foes are more relentless.

Scroll: The hero moves primarily from side to side in the Forest (though he can jump quite high, and the screen will scroll with him); right to left in the Passage; and primarily bottom to top in the Fortress and Castle.

Hero's Powers: As he gets under way, Kage has 3 lives, climbing ability, awesome leaping powers, can throw small Star Knives, and swings a wicked Sword. (Note: When Kage is on the bark of a tree—not its limbs—he is unable to jump.) Whenever Kage grabs a Crystal Ball or one of the Forest Denizens that flits overhead, he earns special powers such as splitting into two invulnerable Kages (though each man does exactly the same as the other), obtaining larger Star Knives, gaining the ability to toss 2 Star Knives in succession or in all directions at once, and being able to take a hit from an enemy without dying (a power signified by Kage's wardrobe turning a different color). If he jumps up and gets a Scroll, dead enemies literally rain from the skies. Note: Though Kage can return to an area through which he's already passed, once his enemies (or Forest Denizens) vanish off-screen, they're gone.

Hero's Weaknesses: Getting struck by enemy blades or projectiles are the only things that will kill Kage.

About Your Enemies: Kage fights Shinobis, the red and blue Ninjas; Yobos, the firebreathing Magic Monks; Genbos, the fiery twins; the 2-sworded Yuki, a Samurai; and the leader of the others, the Samurai Yoshi. Before he begins the second Forest level (that is, after he rescues Kiri and she's kidnapped again), there's a special Forest phase in which Kage must battle invincible White Ninjas. The only way to remove their invulnerability is to slay the Butterfly that passes overhead.

Menu: There is a one-player version, and a two-player version in which Kages fight their own battles on alternating turns.

Timer: None.

Scoring: Points are awarded for obtaining powers and also for killing enemies. These are carefully explained in the game instructions. Overall, remember that *how* you kill an enemy determines how many points you receive: Sword kills earn you more than the safer Star Knife kills.

Patterns: The different areas always look the same. Though Kage's enemies arrive in a slightly different manner and order each time (influenced, also, by what Kage does), they usually come in the same numbers and from roughly the same direction.

Beginner's Strategy: Don't stick around and don't go up into the trees: Simply fire your Star Knives to the left and follow them. The only time you should stop is when you are attacked from the right or need to jump to obtain a Crystal Ball or Forest Denizen. When you reach the Passage level, stay in the water and keep slashing; that will get you safely through (though it *will* be excruciatingly boring!). Follow the black arrow in the Fortress stage, climb the steps, and save the Princess. The easiest way to get through both of the latter levels is with the Star Knives.

Advanced Strategy: There are a pair of fun and challenging ways to earn points in the Forest phase. First: Climb the first tree halfway, and, while jockeying the controller in all directions, attack foes on every side. Second: Go to the right side of the screen, an inch from the edge, and jump up and down, slaughtering enemies as they enter from that side.

Par: 50,000 points for all 4 levels is a good score for someone who presses on without dallying too long in one spot and who uses mostly Star Knives to kill. Remember, though: Kage can really rack up points simply by staying at the early stage of the Forest and killing opponents, especially if he uses his sword.

NES Advantage: A *big* difference will be found by players using the Advantage. Hold down the A button and you're practically invincible, your whirling sword stopping every blade of everyone who approaches. (It won't protect you from fireballs, though.)

Training Tips: Beginners should run through all 4 levels using their Star Knives. They're effective and will allow you to see all the screens. Knowing what you're up against, you can start over and use your blade for more points. For Advanced players, because jumps cover so much ground, leaping with precision is difficult. Practice this in the early phase of the Forest. Also kill using just your blade, without Star Knives or extra powers. If you do well with just your basic Kage, you'll excel when you acquire other weapons.

Rating: Though the game is relatively easy, it's quite enjoyable . . . and there's nothing else quite like it on the market.

Challenge: B
Graphics: B
Sound Effects: B

CHAPTER NINETEEN

MEGA MAN

Type: Science fiction quest.

Objective: In a futuristic world, in the realm known as Monsteropolis, the benign Dr. Wright and his aide, Dr. Wily, constructed the Humanoid robot Mega Man to serve humankind. They also built 6 other Humanoids. Unfortunately, Dr. Wily reprograms them to serve him in a mad effort to take over the world. Only the incorruptible Mega Man stands between Wily and his goal. To win, the superhero must enter the 6 different Empires of Monsteropolis, each of which is governed by a Humanoid and protected by various lackeys. Only by defeating the Humanoids can Mega Man proceed to the seventh Empire for a showdown with Dr. Wily.

Layout: Each of the 7 Empires has its own look, in accordance with the nature of its ruler (snowy and white for Iceman, fiery and red for Fireman, etc.). However, they all have in common a sleek design consisting of vertical and horizontal tunnels, pits, ladders, rooftops, and rooms.

Scroll: Mega Man can move from side to side or up and down as he picks his way through the sprawling Empires.

Hero's Powers: Mega Man begins his quest with the ability to jump and to fire low-potency projectiles. As he vanquishes Humanoids, he acquires their powers (see About Your Enemies, below). He can also collect various Bonuses along the way, which increase his energy or weapon effectiveness. Most important among these are a Magnet Beam generator, which allows Mega Man to create steps in thin air; and Mega Man likenesses that give the player an extra life. Note: When you obtain boosters, you can channel the boost into any power you may have acquired; for example, replenishing your Magnet Beam, blades stolen from Cutman, and so forth.

Hero's Weaknesses: Shots from or collisions with enemies will sap the hero's powers. Falling down shaftways onto spikes or other nasty objects are fatal.

About Your Enemies: The 6 Humanoids each has a particular power: Cutman throws deadly blades, Gutsman heaves and can smash heavy objects, Bombman tosses explosives, Fireman flings fireballs, Elecman discharges electric bolts, and Iceman fires deadly wedges of ice. Dr. Wily has a flying saucer equipped with destructive weapons. There are also many robots and thugs who haunt the Empires and lash out at Mega Man. These are: Bladers, Fleas, Octopus Batteries, Screw Bombers, Watchers, Pengs, Killer Bullets, Flying Shells, Beaks, Bombombs, Foot Holders, and Big Eyes. Most of these foes inhabit more than one Empire (for example, Beaks can be found in the Cutman, Bombman, and Dr. Wily stages; see game instructions for specific distribution). In the Bombman Empire you'll also face Sniper Joe; in Iceman's domain, you'll battle Crazy Razy; and on the Gutsman stage you'll have to duck the flying picks of the Picket Man. These 3 characters all carry shields for protection and are only vulnerable when they move the shields aside (see Beginner's Strategy, below). There is also a fanlike Yashichi that appears now and then and serves no purpose other than to give the player extra points.

Menu: The player can choose to battle the 6 Humanoids in any order, one- or two-player options. In the one-player mode, at game's end you can start all over or you can continue at the Empire where you died, without losing any powers you may have acquired from previous forays. In the two-player mode, the players can continue one another's game or play individual games on alternating turns.

Timer: None. Mega Man can only be stopped when his Energy Meter runs dry. There are a total of 28 power units in each full Energy Meter. Hits from most of the low-level enemies cost only 2 power units. Hits from more powerful figures sap from 4 to 8 units. A player gets 3 Mega Man figures at the beginning of each game.

Scoring: Each foe earns the player a different point total. The low-level flunkies range from 200 to 800 points each; tough-to-kill sorts earn more, such as Sniper Joe (5000 points) and Big Eye (10,000); the Humanoids all fall in the 50,000 to 100,000 point range; and killing Dr. Wily nets you 200,000 points.

Patterns: Nothing changes. The Empires always have the same layout, and your foes always arrive in the same order and in the same numbers. Note: If you reach certain thresholds in each Empire and you die there, your next Mega Man will not be sent back to the beginning of the Empire but will begin at a point not far from where you perished.

Beginner's Strategy: The key to winning at *Mega Man* is to take the Empires in the following order: Gutsman (you'll need his strength), Bombman, Cutman, Iceman (you'll need his ice for Fireman), Fireman, and then Elecman. You can also start by going from Bombman to Cutman to Gutsman, if you wish, since Cutman's blades come in handy and he can be beaten with help from Bombman's bombs. However, you're going to need the Magnet Beam to succeed in Dr. Wily's domain, and when it appears (inside a wall) you'll want Gutsman's powers to get to it.

As for your foes, many of the lesser lackeys can only be killed with a shot in the head or eye. Don't waste fire, for example, on Beaks whose shells are shut. Likewise, don't squander bombs on Spines. They tend to move out of the way too quickly; it's better to use blades. (The one exception is when Spines are diagonal from one another. If you drop the bomb in the right spot, it will neutralize *both* Spines.) Unless you're really battle-hardened *and* point hungry, run under the hopping Big Eyes . . . and keep on running. They'll stomp the inexperienced player flat. In any level, if you find energy boosters lying about, gather them,

95

leave the screen, then duck back in; more boosters will be waiting for you. This is the best way to stock up on power before meeting one of the Humanoids. Knowing the boosters are ahead will also allow you to be a bit more daring when battling the lesser lackeys. Be careful when jumping from Foot Holder to Foot Holder. Just because one of them pulls up beside you, it doesn't mean you should hop right on. For instance, on the Iceman level, if you go right from the second Foot Holder to the third, the one you just left will blast you. Wait until the third Foot Holder comes by for its *next* pass. Pay careful attention, too, to the pattern in which the disappearing steps appear in Iceman's Empire. In the first pit, you'll get out by going up, then diagonally up to the left, followed by a diagonal jump down to the right, a diagonal hop up to the right, a move straight across to the left, a diagonal climb up to the right, a diagonal leap up to the left, then out to the left. In the second pit you'll only need 5 of the 11 steps: take 3 diagonal jumps up to the right, a leap straight up, then a hop to the left, and you're out. In the Bombman Empire you can escape the shrapnel of Bombombs by tucking yourself into the corner formed by the tower and the platform you're on. In the Fireman Empire a *very* important maneuver is the use of ice to get past the 3 shooting columns of flame. Stand at the foot of the first pillar and shoot it *and* the one beyond it when they're low. Hop on top of the frozen fire, shoot the third, and continue on. (You can also hit the first column, then tackle the next two with one blast.) In the Gutsman Empire, when you meet Picket Man, shoot him immediately, just once, and then jump back to avoid his first throw. Whether facing Picket Man or Sniper Joe, keep up a steady barrage. When they get tired of standing around, they'll move the shield to attack you and there will be no avoiding your shots.

Advanced Strategies: A few clues on beating the Humanoids. To defeat Gutsman, stand on the crack between the ledge (on the far left) and the rock next to it. That's your best vantage point for escaping his attack and launching your own. To battle Fireman, use a jump-shoot, jump-shoot pattern. To tackle Cutman, go to the lower level, where he's easier to hit. When he hops up, run under him; when he goes in one direction and you go under him in the other direction, that gives you more time to turn and fire at him. If you have a full Energy Meter when you battle Cutman, just take the cuts he has to give and keep shooting. He'll die before you do. When facing Bombman: his bombs can only hurt you if they're an inch away. Otherwise, he's useless, an easy target if you just keep jumping and firing. When you meet Elecman, stay on the top level of his chamber. It's easier to jump over his bolts from there. Of all the weapons in your arsenal, he is particularly vulnerable to blades. To deal with Iceman: his ice wedges come in threes. In order to clear them all, jump up between the first and second. You'll come down after the third. And be ready to do it again as the next wave approaches. In Wily's domain, you'll need to create steps. Take high jumps before laying in a Magnet Beam step, or you'll run out of energy before reaching the top. When you face the robot, jump its flying body parts while shooting electricity at its eye.

Par: You should earn 200,000 points per empire.

NES Advantage: Slow isn't much help in this game, but the Advantage is *extremely* useful because it gives your stripped-down Mega Man more and faster bullets.

Training Tips: Most players find the precision jumping most difficult; that is, from Foot Holder to Foot Holder, from disappearing step to step, or hopping up and coming down again when moving platforms try to dump you into the ether. When you reach these regions of the Empires, stay there and practice your skills. Also, work on shooting those wicked Big Eyes with just your Mega Man gun. It'll sharpen your marksmanship for any and all other foes.

Rating: This game is exciting for a while, and there's a great deal of terrain to explore. However, once you learn the lay of the land and its ins and outs, the game becomes something of a chore—particularly when you have to wade through the easier foes to get back to more difficult ones.

The visuals of the Empires are excellent, and the animation of the creatures is superb.

Challenge: B
Graphics: A
Sound Effects: C

CHAPTER TWENTY

METROID

Type: Science fiction quest.

Objective: It's the year 2005, half a decade after a cosmic congress known as the Galactic Federation has been established. Peace and contentment reign—until space pirates steal the only known specimen of a Metroid, a life form newly discovered on the world SR388 . . . a creature believed to have wiped out all other life forms on that planet. Fearing that the pirates are going to cause the monster to multiply and send it against the worlds of the Federation, Federation Police dispatch space hunter Samus Aran, a powerful cyborg, to the pirates' planet, Zebes. There, Samus must penetrate the mazes inside the world, avoid monsters and pitfalls, collect various power sources, defeat the Mini-Bosses and Mother Brain, and destroy Metroids.

Layout: The planet's interior is a dark world of caverns and metallic corridors, floating platforms, fiery lava pits, and creatures that flit about or lie in wait. The 5 sections of the alien headquarters are Tourian, Brinstar, Norfair, Mini-Boss Hideout 1, and Mini-Boss Hideout 2.

Scroll: The image moves from side to side or up and down as Samus barrels his way through Zebes.

Hero's Powers: At the start, Samus has just a blaster and the ability to make powerful jumps. Along the way he collects the following weapons and/or power boosters: Maru Mari, which enables him to become a ball and roll through tight spots; the Long Beam, which boosts the range of his gun;

Missiles, which pack far more firepower than his measly laser gun (there are 5 Missiles in each Missile site you capture); an Energy Tank, which allows Samus to store extra energy; Bombs; an Ice Beam, which freezes objects; a Wave Beam, which radiates in several directions at once; High Jump, winged boots that boost the cyborg's leaping capacity by 150 percent; the Screw Attack, a buzzsawlike attribute that allows Samus to spin and slash; and Varia, which diminishes by fifty percent any power loss Samus may suffer. Dead enemies can also provide power or Missile boosts (see About Your Enemies).

Hero's Weaknesses: Contact with anything but the walls, floors, and ceiling costs Samus power.

About Your Enemies: *Metroid* may well be the most thickly populated video game in history. The monsters are Mellows, Zebs, Zoomers, the Skree, Rios, Rippers, Wavers, Memus, Geegas, Zeelas, Side-Hoppers, Mellas, Novae (which are covered with fire-resistant wool!), Gamets, Ripper IIs (tougher than their cousins), Dragons, Violas, Multiviolas, Holtzes, and Dessgeegas. These enemies are all insect- or batlike . . . flying, hopping, or slithering about the caverns. When these enemies die, they may leave behind purple power balls or Missiles, which Samus can collect and add to his arsenal. These remain on the screen for 10 seconds before vanishing. There are also the Mini-Bosses Kraid and Ridley. Kraid fires Missiles from his belly, Ridley spits flame. And, of course, there's the awesome Mother Brain and the Metroids. The latter have the ability to latch on to Samus's body and quickly drain his power.

Menu: There is only the one quest, although you can choose which way you wish to send Samus.

Timer: None. The only way the game will end is when Samus runs out of juice.

Scoring: There is no scoring, only the collection of all-important power units. Samus starts with 30 units and can collect up to 99. With Energy Tanks he can add another 100 per Tank. Samus is permitted to collect just 6 Tanks. (The other item with a cap on it are the Missiles; you can have no more than 255 at any given time.)

Patterns: The layout never chang… the monsters are always located in the same place… such as the Zoomers, move in straight lines, una… …res-ence. Some, like the Rios, have it in for y… will attack.

Beginner's Strategy: To get under way, keep in mi… Zoomers won't bother you if you don't bump int… …, and that to avoid the Skree, simply become a ball (see below) and roll past them (contact with these enemies will cost you 8 power units; dead, the creatures leave behind purple orbs worth 5 power units). When you encounter Rios, jump up (over them, if they're low enough). When Samus jumps, Rios automatically rise; it's easy, then, to get under them and blast them to atoms (4 shots will do the trick). Don't forget that you can also shoot while you jump. This is especially useful when you're simultaneously leaping lava flows and trying to fight Wavers.

Before you do any serious Metroid hunting, you're going to have to roam the underground world to acquire power boosters. You should try to collect them in this order: Maru Mari, Missiles, the Long Beam, an Energy Tank, Bombs, the Ice Beam, more Missiles, another Energy Tank, and Varia. Gathering them in this sequence will give you the firepower you need to negotiate the tunnels and passageways. Naturally, you would be wise to sketch out a map as you move through the maze. (Remember, too, that bombs aren't just for killing, but can also blow holes in walls and floors so that you can make your own doors; and that not only does the Ice Beam paralyze creatures like the Rippers, which cannot be killed, but it can also freeze enemy rays, such as Ridley's fireballs. You can then use these enemy icicles as stepladders, if you wish.) The Maru Mari is almost immediately to your left. After you get it, head right until you reach a vertical blue passage. Ascend to the door on the right, go through, and drop down the vertical gold passage. At the bottom, head right to the Missiles. Backtrack up the gold passage, go left through the door, back to the blue passage, head up, and at the top go left to obtain the Long Beam. Then it's back again to the gold passage. This time,

...ing it horizontally to reach the door ... Go through and continue along the passage right, until you reach the Energy Tank. Get it, however going right, where you'll come to another gold sage. Climb, go through the door on the left, and press onward until you reach the Bombs. At this point return to where you found the Energy Tank. Continue to the left and go through the door. There, descend to the gold passage, head left, and continue until you get the Ice Beam. Backtrack all the way to the gold passage you entered when gameplay began (on the left), ascend, enter the top door on the right, continue right to more Missiles and another Energy Tank, then double back. You'll pass under one set of bricks, then another. When you reach this second set, fire *up* and blast a hole into the level above you. (Note: When you shoot through bricks, you have to jump up through the hole and jockey to the left or right . . . or you'll fall right back down. However, if you have trouble doing this, just keep jumping straight up; eventually the bricks repair themselves and will close beneath you.) Once you're up, move to the left and collect Varia. You're now armed to the teeth. As for the other weapons, the High Jump is located in Norfair. Head to the vertical purple passage to the far right, enter the sixth door down from the top, and head left. The Wave Beam is also in Norfair, in the second tunnel from the bottom, halfway between the vertical center of Norfair and the far-left side. The Screw Attack can be found in Norfair on the far left side of the sixth tunnel from the bottom. In all, there are 19 spots to find Missiles, 6 to find Energy Tanks, and 2 to find Ice Beams.

After you've obtained all of the armaments, head to Brinstar for a showdown with Kraid. Make sure you write down the code that will appear when and if Samus dies; if you punch it into the game when you start over, you'll begin where you left off. Finally, be aware that while it only takes a few blaster shots to get through a blue door, 5 Missiles are required to shoot through a red door.

Advanced Strategy: Once you know the layout of Zebes, the key strategies are defeating the tougher enemies. The best way to fight Metroids is to use the Ice Beam to paralyze them, then kill them with 5 Missiles. If a Metroid grabs you, the best thing to do is to become a ball and leave Bombs. Another problem is getting into Tourian. Actually, there are two shortcuts. After you've beaten the Mini-Bosses, all you have to do is find the pair of statues in Brinstar (top level, far-left side of the tunnel) and hit them with a laser blast. They will grow and allow you to climb to Tourian. The second shortcut: there's a Rio in the chamber adjoining that of the statues. Lure it to just below the statue platform, freeze it, and leap onto its head. Become a ball, drop a bomb, and hop off as the monster explodes. There's a door to the left; go through it and you're in Tourian. It's also possible to boost your gunfire at any point by depressing the B button and the Select button at the same time, and to make a high jump without High Jump by becoming a ball, dropping a bomb, hitting the A button to become full-sized again, and being blasted into the air. As soon as you're launched, do a jump and you'll really go flying. Another neat trick is being able to climb up sheer walls over doors. Open a door, move into the frame, and let the door shut on you. Simultaneously hold down the A button and quickly tap on the control button. You'll hop right up the wall. (To do this with NES Advantage: depress the A button and turn up the Turbo.)

As for Ridley, a quick way to get rid of the fiend is to note which way he's unleashing fireballs. If they're going up, then down, use your ice to freeze them, then hop onto the flaming projectiles and blast Ridley using Missiles. If the fireballs are angling down and away, position yourself as close as you can to the platform on which he's standing and blow him away. Another tactic that works against Ridley is to go into the chamber and position yourself over the rock that's under the blue gate. Open the gate by shooting it, then jump in as it begins to shut. Not only will Samus be protected from Ridley, but he can use Missiles to end the Mini-Boss's murderous career.

Par: Not applicable.

NES Advantage: The Advantage allows your basic gun unit to

fire more rapidly. Otherwise, it isn't a dramatic improvement.

Training Tips: Apart from your shooting skills—which you can polish by staying near the starting point and plugging Zoomers, Rios, and the Skree—you'll need to become proficient at jumping up and down in the vertical passages. Practice this by clearing a passageway of monsters and then just hopping from ledge to ledge. For descents, you should be skimming the ends of ledges as you drop, barely landing on each.

Rating: This game is truly an adventure. There's a lot to discover, a lot to shoot, and a lot that tries to terminate *you*.

Challenge: A

Graphics: B (The scenery is stark, but the animation is nifty.)

Sound Effects: B

CHAPTER TWENTY-ONE

MIKE TYSON'S PUNCH-OUT

Type: Boxing.

Objective: You are the scrappy Little Mac and you're gunning for the heavyweight crown. To get it, you must beat Mike Tyson in the ring. Before reaching Mighty Mike, however, you must battle a series of powerful pugilists in the Minor Circuit, the Major Circuit, and, finally, in the World Circuit.

Layout: The screen shows the ring, the fighters, the ref, and the cheering crowd. Between rounds Mac's trainer, Doc Louis, is seen rubbing the fighter's shoulder and whispering tips, while Mac's adversary flings taunts.

Scroll: None. The fighters have a limited amount of mobility on their respective sides of the ring.

Hero's Powers: Mac has the ability to punch left and right to the face or body, throw an uppercut, dodge to the right or left, block blows, or duck. If Mac goes down, jabbing the B button quickly will help him get up faster. If the Select button is pressed repeatedly between rounds, Mac's stamina will increase. Mac accumulates Stars (displayed in the upper left corner of the screen) each time he connects with a punch. These enable Mac to throw devastating uppercuts.

Hero's Weaknesses: Getting socked drains his power; each hit also causes him to lose a Star, and he surrenders them *all* if he's sent to the canvas. If Mac turns red from having taken a beating, he cannot punch, he can only duck, dodge, and block until he recoups his strength. Mac or his opponent will lose if he: falls 3 times in a round (some lose with 2 falls), or does not get up from the canvas before the count of 10. In the event that both fighters go the distance, the loser is the one judged to have fought a lesser fight (this does not apply to all fighters, however . . . and is blatantly unfair when you're in another man's hometown).

About Your Enemies: Each of your adversaries has one or more specialties. Glass Joe and Von Kaiser go right down. Piston Honda is tougher, with a deadly Piston Punch as well as left jabs, squatting left and right uppercuts, kneeling uppercuts, and a right hook. Don Flamenco has a tough uppercut known as the Flamenco Punch, plus dazzling right hooks. King Hippo hits harder than those who came before, punching straight ahead or down. Great Tiger has a dizzying Magic Punch, not to mention a left jab and squatting left and right uppercuts. Bald Bull goes to the top of the ring and charges with all his might (which is considerable), also relying on quick, rolling jabs, an uppercut, and a right hook. Mr. Sandman strops you with a Razor Uppercut—a series of hard, fast blows—and also packs left and right hooks and jabs. Soda Popinski is known for his speedy jabs, plus left and right uppercuts and hooks. Super Macho Man is famous for his Super Spin Punch, a bone-crunching uppercut. And Mike Tyson is renowned for everything: speed, feints, and power.

The boxers are easiest to beat in the early trials. As you get closer to the title bout, they get tougher: protecting themselves better, punching more frequently and harder, and displaying *much* more stamina. (For instance, Flamenco unveils an eye-closing left jab in the World Circuit.)

Menu: There is only the one-fighter game, in which he faces each foe in turn.

Timer: One minute of game time equals 20 real seconds. Each round is 3 game-minutes; there are 3 rounds per bout.

Scoring: Mac gets 10 points per punch, 100 points when he causes his opponent to see stars, and 1000 points when a foe is knocked to the canvas.

Patterns: The fighters always appear in the same order. Obviously, how you conduct yourself will determine how they punch and whether you get a rematch, are down-ranked, etc.

Beginner's Strategy: The instruction booklet provides basic video-boxing strategies. Thus, we'll concentrate on dealing with the individual fighters.

Glass Joe: A series of punches to the jaw, and he's down.

Von Kaiser: Virtually any combination will do him in, although his gut can take more punishment than his face. Uppercuts are especially effective. Regardless of what you use, keep on punching.

Piston Honda: Strong as he is, Piston telegraphs his haymakers by twitching his eyebrows first. Still them with a punch to the head. Also, when he comes down at you after his little side-to-side dance (he shifts 4 times), he'll always throw an uppercut. Dodge and counterpunch with a rap in the mouth.

Don Flamenco: If you punch him outright, he'll block it and counterpunch. Regardless of who gets things cooking, dodge his big opening uppercut (you'll usually have to go to the left), then introduce his face to a left-right flurry. Repeat as needed to put the rube away. (Early on in the circuit, Don's second trip to the mat will be his last.) Important: Ignore Don's taunts for you to attack him! He'll only greet you with his Flamenco Punch. In later rounds he'll open with jabs, then wait for you to attack. Do so, but be ready to block or dodge his counterpunch.

King Hippo: When he opens his mouth and raises his big fist, bash him in the face. His pants will fall, and when he tries to pick them up, greet him with a flurry of blows to his weakest spot: his navel. Repeat the process and he'll go down.

Advanced Strategy: A general tip: On the World Circuit you can throw super-fast punches after a dodge. Press the controller in the direction *opposite* the way you dodged. Throw your punch, and it'll be faster than usual.

Great Tiger: He always starts with a series of jabs: Watch for them! They begin immediately after his ruby shines! Whenever his left glove (on your right) is extended, hit him with a left to the face. Do the same when he's hunched over, his hands at his belly. As for the Magic Punch—if he's going to use it at all in the first round, it'll appear in the last 40 seconds. (He always opens with it in the second round.) Do *nothing* offensive: simply use a block against it. He'll usually come at you 5 times in succession, and will be dizzy from all the spinning. When he's dazed, unleash a series of left-right blows to his face.

Bald Bull: Whenever he moves his hands quickly up and down, you know a hook is coming. Dodge, and, when his left glove is extended, hit him in the face with a right. When he lets loose a right uppercut, respond with 3 lefts to the face. When he charges you, don't bother dodging (he'll only try again). Instead, give him a left to the stomach on the third of his 3 quick hops. When you face him on the World Circuit level, an uppercut is the most successful way to bring him down.

Mr. Sandman: He always moves his hands rapidly up and down before he throws a hook, and pauses for a lengthy spell before tossing 4 of his numbing uppercuts. Against these and other punches in his arsenal, respond with a smack to the face followed by a series of body punches.

Soda Popinski: You'll know that Soda is about to throw one to 3 jabs when his feet start to move quickly back and forth. When he throws his punch(es)—left or right—dodge or block, then go to his face with your right. You'll be able to land up to a half-dozen blows.

Super Macho Man: When he starts throwing punches, duck to the left and hit him with 4 quick jabs to the face. Reeling, he'll rely on a Super Spin. Go left again, then come back at him, battering him in the face. Be on guard, though, since he'll throw anywhere from one to a dozen Spins during a bout. If he serves you an uppercut, wait until his arm is on the way back, then go for 2 quick jabs to the gut or one to the face. This will usually earn you a Star.

Mike Tyson: Tyson will come at you with his fast flurries, against which your best defense (and subsequent offense) is to dodge left, then quickly answer with a pair of blows to the face. Deal with his feint hooks the same way. You've got to work on tiring him out for the first 2 rounds; this will enable you to score a TKO (though not a knockout) in the third.

Par: You should be able to polish off the first 2 fighters in under a minute, and the other Minor Circuit fighters in under 2 rounds. Most of the Major Circuit figures will usually require just over 2 rounds. Everyone else will take the full 3 rounds to beat.

NES Advantage: No help here; better to wear brass knuckles under your glove.

Training Tips: Go right to Tyson to hone your skills. Do this by punching in the code 007 373 5963.

Rating: The game is entertaining, with a challenge for players of every skill level. The characters and their idiosyncrasies would be amusing . . . if their blows weren't so debilitating!

Challenge: A
Graphics: B
Sound Effects: B

CHAPTER TWENTY-TWO

PRO WRESTLING

Type: Hand-to-hand (and sometimes head-to-canvas) fighting.

Objective: You're one of 6 mighty wrestlers in the Video Wrestling Association, each of whom has several special abilities. Your task is to beat the other 5 fighters so that you can meet the awesome Great Puma for the VWA crown. To win, you must pin the other players for a count of three, or fling them from the ring and keep them out for 20 seconds.

Layout: There's a ring, a referee, the two wrestlers, and a cheering crowd in the background.

Scroll: The picture moves from side to side as the fighters pursue one another. When one of them is heaved from the ring, the screen scrolls in that direction.

Hero's Powers: The 6 rasslers are Fighter Hayabusa, Starman, Kin Corn Karn, Giant Panther, the Amazon, and King Slender. Each has the same 12 basic wrestling moves; each also possesses one patented move of his own. (See game pak instructions for a listing.) They also move in 8 directions, can climb into and out of the ring, can pin an adversary, can try to get out from under a pin, can climb onto the corner post and jump down, and even (if you're slightly daft) help a dazed opponent back into the ring.

Hero's Weaknesses: Getting outmaneuvered and clobbered. An alarm sounds when you're halfway to exhaustion; another blares when you're about to run entirely out of steam.

About Your Enemies: Whoever you are, your common foe is

the Great Puma, who has all the abilities of the other fighters . . . and then some.

Menu: You can fight another opponent or the computer. The rules and gameplay are the same, regardless of which fighter you choose to be.

Timer: Each game against a human foe lasts until one of the fighters falls on his face. Each game against the computer lasts a maximum of 5 minutes. The clock counts down in real time. Note: No matter how much you may bash your computer enemy, if the clock runs out before he does, the game ends in a draw.

Scoring: There are no points, per se. Opponents weaken as they beat the tar from each other.

Patterns: The fighters always start in diagonally opposite corners (left on top, right on bottom).

Beginner's Strategy: When you get knocked down, you'll rise and stand panting and immobile for several seconds. Push your controller on the side *opposite* from where your adversary is standing; you'll want to get the hell out as soon as you can move again. When you get your opponent down, press on the B button; that will force him to get back onto his feet. Whenever possible, use the corner post and jump onto a downed foe. It'll drain him more than simply pinning him. Keep in mind, though, that if you stand poised on the post for more than 5 seconds, you'll be slapped with a technical foul and lose. Also, don't do this until your opponent is really ragged. Otherwise, it's easy for him to roll out of the way. Hurl yourself against the ropes whenever possible, for added clout when you strike a foe. However, never let yourself be backed against the ropes. Your fighter won't have enough room to do any kicking.

Advanced Strategy: There's one sure-fire way to win: select Fighter Hayabusa, fell your opponent with a Back Brain Kick, and pin them. When you both rise, give the controller two taps so Hayabusa is back up, then tap it again and move in, give your hated foe another Back Brain Kick, pin them once more and repeat. After 15 of these, you're the champ. Even the computer falls for this tack. As for the Great Puma, the big, golden, two-legged feline will *not* be brought down by repeated Back Brain Kicks. In fact, nothing short of a laser from *Gradius* will hurt him. Your best chance of winning is to toss him from the ring and carry the fight out there. Remember: All you need to do is keep him out there for 20 seconds.

Par: Most players can beat the 5 other wrestlers, but whipping Puma is no day at the beach. A good player should be able to end a normal match in 2:10. It will take a relentless fighter a *minimum* of 4 minutes to tire Puma.

NES Advantage: Most players find the joystick easier to use than the basic controller. Otherwise, there are no advantages.

Training Tips: Play the two-player game alone, practicing maneuvers with each wrestler.

Rating: This one's a lot of fun. What's more, depending upon who your opponent is, it's always different. It would have been nice if the scenery could have changed, or if there were more than just one specialty per fighter. Still, this is a great party cartridge.

Challenge: B+
Graphics: B
Sound Effects: B

CHAPTER TWENTY-THREE

RAD RACER

Type: Auto race.

Objective: It's a Cannonball Run, of sorts, as you tear through 8 different locales: Stage 1 is "Sunset Coastline"; Stage 2, "San Francisco Highway" (at night); Stage 3, "Grand Canyon"; Stage 4, "Ruins of Athens"; Stage 5, "Los Angeles Night Way"; Stage 6, "Snow White Line" in the Rockies; Stage 7, "Seaway in Typhoon"; and Stage 8, "Last Seaside Running."

Layout: The point-of-view is from behind the car you're driving.

Scroll: The picture moves toward you. As you steer, the lanes and horizon move from side to side.

Hero's Powers: In addition to accelerating, braking, and steering, players can engage Turbo-speed by pushing the controller ahead once 100 Km/h has been achieved. This enables you to reach a maximum speed of 255 Km/h. Careful drivers can also nudge other cars aside and use them for a slingshot maneuver (see Advanced Strategy, below).

Hero's Weaknesses: Crashing into obstacles on the side of the road, or into the rear ends of cars while going at top speed (especially on later levels, such as Stage 5), will total your vehicle, costing precious time while another is brought in (5 seconds are wasted when you're wrecked; 3 seconds more go by as you get back to 100). Other cars can butt you to the side and off the road.

About Your Enemies: Traffic gets pushier as the levels change.

Moreover, in each stage there are bothersome standouts. In Stage 1 you face very manageable Volkswagen bugs; Stage 2, a Corvette; Stage 3, a Citroen; Stage 4, a Mercedes; Stage 5, a Lamborghini that *doesn't* want you to pass; Stage 6, a Lotus; Stage 7, a Porsche; and Stage 8, a road-hog Testarossa.

Menu: You can select either a 328 Twin Turbo or FI. There's no difference between the cars, save for their appearance. Selecting a car also changes the look (though not the patterns) of the other vehicles you'll encounter.

Timer: Each initial round lasts 45 seconds, counting down in real time. The time on bonus rounds depends upon how far you got on the previous round (see Scoring).

Scoring: You earn points for each kilometer you pass. Garner enough points and the clock is reset. (That's the only way you'll be able to complete any of the courses.)

Patterns: Though each course is different from the next, the roads are always the same from game to game, as are the order in which the cars appear (obviously, your own interaction with traffic—slowing, passing, crashing—will change the latter to a degree).

Beginner's Strategy: The cornerstone to winning is passing, and passing is achieved by pushing the brake lightly when you're behind the car you want to pass, pacing it for a moment, then zooming around it. (You can also stay behind the other car for a few moments, letting *it* lead you through traffic. Stay behind it, though, and you lose time.) This brake-and-dart tactic is especially important when cars are traveling abreast and blocking the road. You'll need the braking delay to see which one's going to pull ahead and give you an opening. On *any* curve, don't slow completely: *Tap* the brake just enough to hold the turn, *then* burn rubber. Things to watch out for on the early courses are as follows:

Stage 1: The cars are not terribly aggressive here. All you have to watch out for are curves, which occur mainly at the beginning and toward the end. To get under way, keep the accelerator down so you'll shoot down the road; when you reach 100, bring Turbo to bear and go to the left. Weave through the first 2 cars you encounter; don't slow until you pass through the next 2 cars. They'll be on either side as you enter a curve. Brake to approximately 200, slip through the cars as you take the curve, and continue ahead.

Stage 2: The first 3 cars you see will be blocking you in. Go to the left; brake-and-dart to the left of the car in the middle. Get into the center lane, in front of it, and remain there to get past the next cars.

Stage 3: This one opens easy—but watch out for a hairpin curve (at approximately 29 on the Timer, assuming Turbo speed). Be careful of riding on the shoulder, since the rocks are not as visible as the trees, signs, etc., in other stages.

Stage 4: Traffic is sparse to start, and the curves are relatively smooth in the beginning. Toward the end, however, there are 8 maddening curves in a row! Shift rapidly from side to side as you take these.

Advanced Strategy: Overall, there's a way to take curves at top speed, but it's a precision move that'll cost you a lot of cars before you get it down. To turn *right,* tag the left side of the fender of a car in front of you, using the right side of your fender. That'll nudge you around. To go left, hit your front left fender against the other driver's rear right side. As for specific courses:

Stage 5: The Lamborghini is a *very* pushy car. It does not want you to pass, and will push you to the side of the road whenever possible. A good bet is to tailgate the Lamborghini and dart around it whenever the road straightens. There are some serious curves toward the middle and the end of this course.

Stage 6: The road is very empty to start . . . but then the cars (and curves) come up quickly. Toward the end there are a pair of right-angle turns that will send you into a snowbank if you don't take them slowly.

Stage 7: For such a late stage, this is surprisingly mild. Though the road is serpentine, the cars aren't as pushy as in Stage 5.

Stage 8: The Testarossa is the archetypical road hog. After passing your first car (the blue one; go by it on the left), as with the Lamborghini, tailgate, then brake-and-dart.

Par: In Stage 1 you must be in no more than 3 crashes to get all the way through; 2 crashes in Stage 2; one in Stage 3; and none in any others. Most drivers are able to make it through Stage 4.

NES Advantage: The joystick is considerably better than the controller, allowing you to make more precise shifts in your course. Since the joystick is more like a stick shift, many players also find this more "realistic."

Training Tips: Watch the display screens of every stage, and also practice your skills on the toughest levels. How do you get there without making it through the early phases? Simple. When the car-selection screen appears, press Start. Look at the tachometer (the bars above the distance-covered indicator). Tap the B button; you will add 2 bars with each tap. Each successive set of 2 bars indicates the next successive stage. When you've got the stage you want, push the controller up and to the right, then press Start. You will automatically hop to that level. If you lose and want to remain at that level, wait until the display screen returns *(not* the course screen). Press A and hold it down when you push Start. (Note: To get to the entertaining finale of the game, use the tachometer procedure . . . only hit the B button 63 times before shifting the controller.)

Rating: Knockout graphics—Frisco and L.A. at night are miracles!—responsive controls, your choice of music (!), and breakneck pace make this a delight. The 3-D mode is just okay, though; you have to turn the brightness *way* up, and even then, the only real depth you get is between the road and the horizon. There's practically no dimension to the cars or obstacles, and the L.A. skyline is totally dim. Nonetheless, the 2-D *Rad Racer* is a classic!

Challenge: A

Graphics: A+

Sound Effects: A

CHAPTER TWENTY-FOUR

RUSH 'N ATTACK

Type: Military search-and-destroy.

Objective: Inside a fortified military base are American POWs. A crackerjack soldier, you (and an ally, if you choose) must penetrate 5 theaters of combat before you can storm the Enemy Base.

Layout: The terrain you cover is the Iron Bridge and Missile Base, the Airport, the Harbor, the Forest and Hangar, the Warehouse, and finally, the Base.

Scroll: The hero(es) move from left to right.

Hero's Powers: You get under way with 5 lives (you collect more as points accrue), the power to leap, and the ability to stab while standing up or lying on your belly. (Even if you're on the ground and stab a foe in the foot, he dies.) Every time you draw upon a new life, you have a second of invincibility, and each time you kill a *reclining* yellow soldier (even after he's gotten up and run at you), you acquire either a 3-shot Bazooka, 3 Hand Grenades (they don't kill everyone on the screen, just enemies in their immediate vicinity), a Pistol with unlimited ammo (unfortunately, it vanishes after 15 seconds), or an Invincibility Shield (which lasts for 10 seconds). Each new acquisition supplants the one you gathered before it, even if you haven't used it. When you move from one level to another, you automatically lose your weapon.

Hero's Weaknesses: Touching an enemy, being shot, or stepping on a Mine will put you in a body bag.

About Your Enemies: There are 9 general types of enemies: Foot Soldiers (several varieties), Jumping Soldiers, Pistol Soldiers, Machine Gun Soldiers, Paratroopers (they become Machine Gun Soldiers when they land), Artillerymen, Rocket Men, Autogyro Pilots, and Dogs. Most just run off the screen; a few—such as yellow Foot Soldiers (which first appear in the Airport level) follow you around.

Menu: One- and two-player versions.

Timer: None.

Scoring: You receive a minimum of 100 points (for capturing a weapon), 200 to 300 points for killing Foot Soldiers, 1000 points for Jumping Soldiers, 2000 for Rocket Men, and so on. You earn the same amount of points regardless of the weapon you use to kill; nor does it make any difference whether you are standing or are on your belly.

Patterns: The terrain and arrival of the soldiers is always identical (though if you climb to the top of a structure, more soldiers will descend on that tier than if you had remained on the ground). Likewise, the location and number of reclining soldiers and their weapons caches are identical in both the one- and two-player games.

Beginner's Strategy: In general, you can kill Jumping Soldiers by leaping up when they do and stabbing them in midair. Just make sure there isn't a Mine on the other side of them. Watch out for *any* soldiers when you cross a Minefield: since they can't be killed by Mines, you could be in mid-hop and come down right in the arms of an enemy. When you start out, stay on the ground level; you'll need to get the Bazooka. You can use it to blast the 3 Mines, if you like: lie down as close as possible to the first Mine, shoot over it, then get up *fast* and run. If you hustle, causing the screen to scroll quickly, your Bazooka shell will detonate all 3 Mines. As you proceed past the Missile Launchers, use your knife to kill enemies on your level; meanwhile, jump up and fire Bazooka shells at the Jumping Soldiers atop the missile launchers. The second reclining soldier on this level also packs a Bazooka. When the siren sounds (as you reach the sixth cannon after the missile launchers), head to the left of the screen and face right. You will face 3 waves of soldiers:

118

Use the second Bazooka to blast each wave as the lead soldier is almost upon you.

On the Airport level the first reclining soldier will provide you with a Bazooka, the second with Grenades. Things get a bit tricky when you reach the 5 guard towers before the end of the airstrip. You should mount trucks, first, and use the Bazooka to kill the first 2 gunners up there. Otherwise you'll have a tough time dodging bullets *and* fighting Jumping Soldiers. Be careful, though, when you leap off trucks: If an enemy is nearby and scoots over, and you land on him, you lose a life. When the siren sounds, Rocket Men descend. You can jump up and kill them *or* you can go to the lower left-hand corner of the screen: the airborne attackers can't get you there. You will, however, have to stab anyone on the ground who tries to kill you (especially from the left).

Advanced Strategy: On the third level the reclining soldiers give you a Star, a Gun, and Grenades, in that order. The Grenades are particularly useful when you reach the end of one stack of bins and are about to cross to the front of another. Hurl them ahead of you, since things tend to be particularly crowded at these junctures. When you hear the siren, lie down in the middle of the screen, shooting right. A half-dozen Dogs will rush at you from this direction, followed by 6 from the left, 6 more from the right, 6 from the left, and finally 3 from both directions (one right, one left, one right, one left, etc.). Just keep punching that "stab" button or you're Puppy Chow.

On the fourth level—and, indeed, on all subsequent levels—strategy isn't as important as rapid reflexes, since enemies of all kinds hail from every direction. The Paratroopers arrive now, drifting to and fro and shooting at you as they descend . . . while you must still deal with soldiers on the ground. When the Autogyros swoop in, wait until they come low, then jump up and stab them as you did the Rocket Men. Note: Make sure you use your Bazooka to detonate the Mines in front of the fence at the mountains on the fourth level. There's an underground complex you'll want to enter. Also: Play the two-player version with one player. Let soldier number 2 die right away; if *your* man

119

dies, then, he will not start as far back as if you were playing in the one-player mode.

Par: You should be averaging 60,000 points for each level, especially in the higher-point, more densely populated later levels.

NES Advantage: The Advantage capacity for rapid-fire stabbing comes in handy . . . especially with the Dogs.

Training Tips: Stabbing is easy; jumping and stabbing together, with precision, takes practice. Work on this, remaining on the first level—where attacks are moderately spaced —and moving ahead only when no more soldiers come to attack. By the time you get to the crowded third level, you'll be glad you mastered these skills.

Rating: The game offers solid, if unsurprising, adventure.

Challenge: B

Graphics: B

Sound Effects: C+

CHAPTER TWENTY-FIVE

SOLOMON'S KEY

Type: Fantasy quest.

Objective: *Solomon's Key* is a book written ages ago by the ruler and great mage. Having developed a formula to rid the world of devils and evil, he put it in the book . . . which he hid. Alas, a curious monk found the volume and released many of the demons. Now, under orders from King Yutra of the fairy realm Lyrac, the wizard Dana must find *Solomon's Key* and restore peace and beauty to the world. To do this, he must race from room to room—obtaining a Key in each and using it to unlock the door to the next.

Layout: The screen is a succession of chambers, with Hidden Rooms accessed by grabbing the Constellation Symbol in every fourth chamber.

Scroll: The plucky wizard can move any way he wishes inside a room.

Hero's Powers: Your hero starts out with 3 lives, the ability to jump one Block-length in any direction (including over the head of an oncoming demon), fall any distance without being hurt, smash golden Blocks with his wand (or, if they're above, by "butting" them repeatedly with his head), *create* Blocks with the wand, and also hover. (This is not mentioned in the instruction booklet: you can levitate, briefly, by jumping up and quickly tapping the A button. You can also levitate *down*, slowly, by jumping and simultaneously using the wand to create a vertical wall of bricks.

This is particularly useful, for example, if you wish to hold back the Ghost in the third room.)

As Dana roves about, he can acquire: a Mamda jar, which allows him to let loose a Fireball that will travel the length of the screen and kill almost anything; the larger Jar of Magadora, which permits him to fire a Superfireball (and will kill not just the first creature it strikes, but will continue rolling, slaying others); the Scroll of Lyra, which permits Dana to stockpile Fireballs beyond normal limits; the Crystal of Rad (a rad crystal indeed!), which extends the reach of Fireballs; the Hourglass of Norm, which adds time to Dana's life; the Medicine of Meltona, which kills every foe on the screen; the Medicine of Edlem, which boosts Dana's strength; the Medicine of Mapros, which gives Dana an extra life; and the incredible Bells of Lyrac, which call Fairies, who bestow an extra life. Dana has the ability (also not revealed in the instructions) to strike a Jewel with his wand, which will change it into a succession of other objects, allowing him to select whichever one he needs.

Hero's Weaknesses: Getting hit by a monster or its flames will make Dana a late wizard.

About Your Enemies: The creatures Dana must face are Demonsheads, monstrous faces which roam about (and are destroyed by collisions with Blocks); Goblins, which can't march down Blocks, only across them; Saramandors and Dragons, flame breathers; Gargoils (sic), whose fire can penetrate Blocks (but who die when dropped onto Blocks); Ghosts, which only move from side to side and die when they hit a Block; Neuls, batlike Ghosts that move up and down; Sparkling Balls, which slither along Blocks—up, down, under, and over—Burns, the living fire; and Panel Monsters, gargoyles that spit Fireballs.

Menu: There is only the one quest, and it'll take you longer to solve than it took Odysseus to return to Ithaca. Even a very good player will require at least 3 months to pick through the rooms and secrets of *Solomon's Key*.

Timer: In each room, Dana has 10,000 time units to complete his chores. In real time, this is 3 minutes.

‥ing: You build your score by collecting Coins, Treasure

Bags, and Jewels. Monsters turn into lucre when they die by means other than falling from a Block.

Patterns: All of the demons, goods, and Blocks are in the same place in each room every time you enter it. However, as you begin building Blocks and killing foes, things change.

Beginner's Strategy: Most beginners make the doomed-to-fail error of trying to outrun monsters. Not only is this bad math—there's an infestation of them, and just one of you—but you'll run out of time. It's better to observe and out-think them. An overview of how to survive the first 5 rooms follows. Once you get the hang of it, getting farther will be relatively easy. Bear in mind that these are not the *only* ways to win . . . just among the safest. Warning: Don't accidentally Fireball the Fairy. She's as vulnerable as your enemies!

Room One: Hit the Block to the right, then the next Block over. Your foe will fall to its death, after which you can ascend one side of the upper room—capturing the goods behind the Blocks midway up—build a bridge across the room to the Bell, and descend the other side—again, collecting powers from the Blocks—before going to the Key room. After grabbing it, go down and out.

Room Two: You begin on the bottom platform. Go up 2 levels, hit the first brick on top to get powers, then continue to the Key. Build a platform to the Bell, cut out a Block and drop down to third level, hit the first Block in the row (on the left) to obtain the Medicine of Meltona, and kill every Demonshead on the screen. Get rich and head for the door. (Note: In the beginning, Demonsheads will stalk you. Don't forget, though, they're not homing monsters; they move in one direction only. Just stay out of their way or vault over them!)

Room Three: Wait until the Panel Monster fires. When the Fireball has passed, put a Block in the right-hand corner. Levitate and whack the Block on the right, go through to the next room, and wait until the Sparkling Balls are at the 7:00 and 9:00 position before scurrying through. Destroy the Block on the far right, drop, and hit the Blocks on the bottom left to get the goods therein. Go through the corridor and enter the next room when the Ghost is on the left. (You can drop or you can levitate down, as described in Hero's Powers, above.) As the Ghost heads right, quickly build a diagonal bridge to the Key, go back down, then hit your way through the row of gold Blocks—jumping back onto your platform when the Sparkling Ball emerges from its dank little pit. Continue on, Fireballing the Goblin, using your head to butt the Block and the monster on top of it, getting the Bell, and building a bridge diagonally to the right. Wait until the 2 firebreathers are superimposed, then zap them with a single Fireball and head for the door.

Room Four: Erect a bridge diagonally to the top of the room, get the Constellation Symbol (your "key" to the Hidden Room), then hop to one of the permanent stones below and fall straight to the bottom (if you can grab the Key as you plummet, so much the better). Build a bridge up toward the Block, just below center, with the Sparkling Ball on it, staggering the bottom 2 Blocks as you ascend, then plugging a Block under the permanent Block: This will divert the monster to the right, so it won't bother you. Come back and butt the Block just above the floor on the left (otherwise, the demon there will trouble you when you build your bridge), then go back up, get the Key, and make yourself a platform toward the 4 permanent Blocks that lie beneath the door. Where a fifth Block would be, on the right, leave a pit. Duck into it when the Goblin heads in your direction. When he turns and shambles to the left, run like the blazes for the door. You'll be borne, by the power of the Constellation, to the Hidden Room. Make sure you smash as many Blocks as possible. Otherwise, you're going to become toast in—

Room Five: This chamber can be easy, or it can be hell . . . literally. Because the Panel Monsters are in staggered rows, one or the other will charbroil you as you ascend. If you got the Jar of Magadora in the Hidden Room, send a Superfireball screaming up one side. An entire wall of Panel Monsters will perish, and it's a cinch, then, to build a bridge and climb. If you *didn't* get the Jar, you'll have to use balls to destroy one monster, make a Block and climb, destroy a demon on the opposite wall, climb, and so on. Your timing must be precise or you'll never make it.

Once you've made it through these rooms you'll be well on your way to mastering the first half of the game. A few tricks you'll want to remember: Against Burns, you can stand on the edge of a Block, facing the monster, and not be hurt. This is useful in a room such as 10, where you must leap one to get the key. Also: Standing on the edge of a Block, facing outward, you can cast a Block farther than normal, a full 2 Block-lengths away.

Advanced Strategy: By the time you reach the later rooms you'll be relying heavily on Blocks to imprison monsters or protect yourself. For example, you *could* use a Superfireball to kill the Sparkling Balls in the central nook in room 11. Better, however, to release them and hide yourself in a small, walled-in area you'll have built below. In room 17 you'll want to use bricks to divert them, sending them off to the left so you can leave the right-hand corner. (In case you *need* a Superfireball, by the way, you'll find one in room 14, second row from the top, third Block from the left.) It's wise to save your weapons for those demons that can disintegrate Blocks. Again, there are numerous ways to go through each room. Whatever route you map, the key to winning the game is to snatch the Stars of David (that is, Solomon's Seal) which are hidden in rooms 9, 13, 17, 19, 21, 29, 46, and 47; and, also, the jewels in rooms 20 and 44. Obtaining these will allow you to get a look at the enchanted book and triumph with a minimum of suffering.

Par: Scores vary wildly, because some players get through multiple rooms with one Dana while many will require all 3 Danae to survive the first chamber. Suffice to say it should take no more than 2000 time units for a good player to clear rooms one through 10 of goods and escape. For rooms 11 through 23, 3000 per chamber is a very good time. For the last half of the game, anyone who keeps half their life time is doing just fine.

NES Advantage: The big plus with the Advantage is being able to hold down the A button and create Blocks rapid fire.

That's particularly valuable if you're facing a Block-busting monster and need to delay it while you look for a way out.

Training Tips: Don't bother studying the map that comes with the game: You can't see much, and many of the monsters aren't pictured. When you reach each new screen, take a moment to look at the monsters and see how they move. Then hit the Pause button and study the terrain; map out the best route to the Key and the door.

Rating: This is a difficult but ultimately fulfilling epic, beautifully made with an entrancing air of mysticism and magic.

Challenge: A

Graphics: A

Sound Effects: A

CHAPTER TWENTY-SIX

SPY HUNTER

Type: Race and shoot.

Objective: As the CIA's greatest secret agent, you have a most important assignment: to stay alive. At the wheel of your sports car—and, later, slapping waves with your motorboat—you must outrace and outshoot the enemy.

Layout: The terrain changes from roads that wind through trees and rivers to the open sea as you elude countless assassins.

Scroll: The player watches from above as the car moves vertically.

Hero's Powers: To start, your car has speed, brakes, maneuverability, and bullets. It also has super-reinforced sides to butt other cars off the road. However, each time you drive into the back of a passing Weapon Van, you can acquire Oil to create oil slicks; Smoke for smoke screens; and Missiles to shoot down enemy Helicopters. The contents of each Van are marked on the roof. (These powers are limited, so use them sparingly!) Extra cars are awarded as often as you need them before time runs out. If you reach a score of 10,000 before the clock ticks off, you are awarded an extra car; extra vehicles are thereafter given at 30,000 point plateaus. You can earn up to 5 spare cars. On the water your G-6155 Interceptor is equipped with whatever weapons you were carrying on your car when you drove into the boathouse. Note: Weapons can be stockpiled. To access different armaments, use the Select button.

Hero's Weaknesses: Your spying days are over if you get shot, knocked off the road, or collide with another car or a piece of scenery (though you can drive on road shoulders, which only slow you down).

About Your Enemies: On the road you must face Tire Slashers, blue cars whose 4 wheels sprout whirling blades (they don't emerge until the car has been on the screen for 5 seconds . . . so you have time to accelerate and race around them); Limousines, whose passengers spray your car with gunfire; Bulletproof Bullies, whose armor makes them impervious to your guns; and Helicopters, which dog you like pesky mosquitoes and drop bombs. Even if the bombs miss you, they leave craters: if you or any other car runs into these, it's beddy-bye. Craters can be hit more than once, so watch out! There are also motorcyclists, red cars, and pale blue cars. These mere motorists offer no threat, unless you happen to collide with them. The road itself is often a hazard, serving up puddles that displace you slightly to one side or the other and ice that causes you to skid. On the high seas you must deal with Speed Boats, which toss oil barrels into the water and explode on contact; and Cruise Boats, which have a pair of torpedo tubes in the rear and in the front.

Menu: There is only the one race game for one player.

Timer: The clock starts at 999 and ticks down. In real time, that's one minute 7 seconds.

Scoring: You drive along to collect as many miles as possible. While the timer remains constant, regardless of your speed, the miles you accrue add up faster the faster you go. Thus, if you crawl along, you won't reach the 10,000 point level before time runs out. That's fine . . . as long as you don't lose the car you're driving.

Patterns: The road is always the same (see Advanced Strategy, below), and both the Weapon Vans and Helicopters usually arrive at the same time and place. For example, the Weapon Van with Smoke is always on the right side of the ~~f...f....~~ the Oil Van on the left. The Helicopter usually ~~....~~ ou cross the first bridge after the second fork. A ~~....~~ ck usually arrives just before or after you face the first chopper. The traffic also passes in a pattern, though you disrupt that as soon as you get on the road. With the exception of Weapon Vans, vehicles that pass you and leave off the top of the screen are gone. You won't see them there when you speed up. However, vehicles you pass have a nasty habit of sneaking up behind you (which is why God invented Oil slicks).

Beginner's Strategy: The key to winning this game is to watch *not* your car, but the top of the screen, right by the mileage counter. That's where the cars are coming from, and it will give you time to adjust your course (you don't have to be watching your car for that, all you need to do is move the controller). Apart from this, there are several things to remember. When you wreck your car, a van comes along and gives you a new one—always dropping you on the right side of the road. When you pull away, make sure your *left* side is clear! Many good but hasty spies are done in by these collisions. Also: When you enter a Weapon Van, do so on the *right* side of the road. Otherwise, the Van will waste precious seconds driving over to that side.

As for self-defense, apart from weaving and dodging as you drive, there are some basic tips to avoiding enemies. Never let a car remain ahead of you as you enter a section where the road narrows. Bulletproof Bullies go faster, for instance, than red cars. If a Bully is on the left and you're on the right, you may well be boxed-in when a red car suddenly appears in front. There won't be time to shoot it, and the rear-ender will be fatal. Also, don't use your guns until you earn your first extra car. It slows you down and you may not reach that 10,000 point plateau in time. When you face a Bulletproof Bully, feint to the side that has the least amount of room between the car and the shoulder. The Bully will skew in that direction, at which point you dart around it in the opposite direction. When a Slasher appears, just speed up and go around it. It won't do anything until the blades pop out. As for the Limousines, their bullets have a limited range; simply keep your distance when passing. The Helicopters are a problem, since they hover above you. When the first one appears, pour on the juice

129

and then brake when it catches up to you. It'll drop a bomb, you'll dash around the crater, and that will be that. Later birds can't be shaken so easily, and the best thing to do is to hang back, wait until they drop a bomb, dash around them, then wait again. While you're waiting for them to unload on the road, keep your guns blazing to shoot any cars that may be ahead of you. You'll want the coast to be clear for your impending departure. Be advised that if you crash when a chopper is just arriving, it usually leaves. Lastly, don't forget that you can use your Smoke to protect your sides as well as your rear. As you pass a vehicle, give a squirt: Smoke will fan out and push your enemy off the road.

Advanced Strategy: Macho drivers dispute this scenario, but it's more or less guaranteed to get you to the boats and beyond. Race like hell in the early phase, until you get your first extra car. When you do, take it *very* slowly. Since time is no longer a factor, and since you no longer have an unlimited supply of cars, use your guns liberally now to blast cars in front of you, instead of trying to race around them. With 2 cars, a careful player will reach those 30,000 point levels and get the full complement of vehicles. Also, *don't* go into a Weapon Van when it first arrives. If you go in, it disappears. If you don't, it'll stay on the road, close by, forcing other cars aside. Ultimately it'll even get testy and try to knock you off the road. *That's* when you accept its weapon. Or, go into the Van when the chopper arrives. You can't be hurt when you're inside.

As you play, you'll notice that the road forks many times. Most routes will get you to the boat level. However, 5 routes will bring you back to earlier points in the game. Take any road to the second river. When you've passed over, stay to the left of whatever road you're on. That will bring you to a narrow road that cuts off sharply to the upper right. This road leads directly to the boathouse. The most direct route from the starting point is to take the first 4 left forks. The road to the right will appear immediately after you take the fourth fork. When you reach the waterways, your guns will be much more important than they were on the road—it's important, obviously, to sink your enemy before they can use their own weapons. Finally, the most important aspect of the game is this: wait 15 seconds at the beginning, leaving your car sitting on the side of the road. That way, the bloody "Peter Gunn" music will *stop* playing and you won't lose your mind. (No, you can't just turn down the volume. If you do, you won't hear the sound of the Helicopter approaching.)

Par: You should have earned your first extra vehicle by the time you reach the first bridge.

NES Advantage: Without question, the joystick is more responsive than the controller. Unfortunately, Slow doesn't work on this game.

Training Tips: This one's neat. When the van drops you off at the beginning of the game, don't race off; stay behind it, allowing it to run block for you as you get a look at the road. It's a terrific way to map the terrain.

Rating: This is a fast, difficult game. Warning: Don't play it and then get into your car. You don't get another car when you crash into real obstacles.

Challenge: A
Graphics: A
Sound Effects: D

CHAPTER TWENTY-SEVEN

TOP GUN

Type: Flight combat simulation.

Objective: When an unnamed enemy threatens U.S. forces near "vital oil fields," you—as an Air Force lieutenant—are ordered to take up your squadron of F-14s and stop the foe on the land, sea, air . . . and even in space! You must also land your fighter safely on the aircraft carrier USS Enterprise, and beginning with phase 2, you must also refuel in midflight.

Layout: The screen shows the terrain and enemy hardware as seen from the cockpit of your plane. Displayed at the bottom of the screen are an altimeter, air speed indicator, fuel meter, artificial horizon, damage indicator, radar, ammunition counter, and missile sight.

Scroll: The on-screen elements come toward you.

Hero's Powers: Each of the 3 planes you can select is extremely maneuverable and fires an unlimited supply of bullets. All have a damage-indicator to show how many bullets have struck you; an altimeter; a gunsight; radar (planes are dots, ships are circles); a fuel meter; an airspeed indicator; a missile-counter; and a horizon indicator. How many missiles you have, and their potency, depends upon the aircraft: the T-11 carries 40 relatively low-power projectiles; the T-22 stocks 20 missiles that pack twice the punch; and the T-33 carries 10 missiles with 4 times the zing.

Hero's Weaknesses: Getting shot 12 times with bullets, hit with a missile, running out of fuel (for example, missing your refuel linkup), or failing to land squarely on the deck of your carrier, will send you down in flames. Lose 3 planes and the game is over.

About Your Enemies: In different phases you must face 5 kinds of enemy airplanes, an attack chopper, 3 seagoing vessels, a submarine, a tank, trucks, artillery and missile launchers, and finally, a space shuttle. Each fires projectiles of one kind or another.

Menu: There is only a one-player game with 4 missions. These must be tackled in turn; there's no jumping ahead.

Timer: None.

Scoring: You earn points for each enemy plane, ship, missile, or vehicle you reduce to a mound of twisted metal (see Par, below).

Patterns: The planes, ships, etc., always come at you in the same sequence, along the same patterns. Most planes come at you in groups of 3.

Beginner's Strategy: There are two keys to getting through the combat phase of the game: being able to duck enemy fire, and learning to read your radar. Ducking is simply a matter of dropping low, climbing, or sliding left or right so that a missile passes off the screen. The trick to using the radar effectively is to rise when blips are in front of you and to descend when blips are behind you. In the latter case, when you drop, they'll pass over you; when the blips are just in front of your jet, shoot up and you'll be right on their tails. As for enemies coming up behind you, these are easily shaken by jockeying all the way to one side, then to the other, then back again. Like magic, the enemy will be gone.

When using the T-11 (which you should, on the first 2 missions), keep in mind that one missile will destroy everything but the Battle Cruisers on mission 2. They require 2 strikes each. Also be aware that submarines always fire 3 missiles in a row. Get rid of those sharks before they have a chance to attack! When it comes to landing, the most important aspect is to keep your speed within a 20 mph range of 300. If you are in that 280 to 320 mph window, and follow the "left," "right," "down," etc. instructions of your on-board computer, you'll land with no trouble. Note: The

133

refueling stage will be necessary at roughly 4 minutes into the second mission. Hit the Start button to summon the tanker plane. You will have just under one minute to dock: Keep your speed and your nose up (regardless of what the computer says), pay attention to the "left, right" instructions, and get the pipe as low as you can on your radar screen. Docking replenishes your missiles as well as your fuel.

Advanced Strategy: Instead of getting out of the way of missiles, blast them. It takes nerves of steel, but a few bullets will do the trick. One missile is easy enough; go from top to bottom or vice versa when there's 3 (if you miss the one on the end, you can always dodge it). Don't try to take out missiles with missiles, since there isn't time to sight and launch. The trick to dealing with the fighters—the planes that slash diagonally across your screen—is to push your controller in the direction they're traveling, track them for just a moment, and release a missile. On mission 3 you'll need 16 missiles to destroy the missile silo, while on mission 4 you *must* knock out the chopper at once. Otherwise it will stay on your tail, firing all the while. Your final target, the shuttle, requires a score of missiles to destroy.

Par: A good score is 12,000 for knocking out enemies, plus another 10,000 for landing safely and 50,000 for a successful refueling.

NES Advantage: You can hold the A or B button down to accelerate or decelerate . . . but so what? Most players prefer the controller to the Advantage joystick.

Training Tips: Keep going back through the first mission until not a single plane gets past you. Otherwise you really won't be ready for the later missions . . . especially the third and fourth. Note: There is no way to jump ahead to those tougher battles. You simply have to slog your way through.

Rating: This visual treat creates a real sensation of flight. The combat situations are entertaining, though there isn't a *whole* lot of variety.

Challenge: B

Graphics: A

Sound Effects: A

CHAPTER TWENTY-EIGHT

URBAN CHAMPION

Type: Hand-to-hand combat.

Objective: You're being picked on by the neighborhood bully. The two of you engage in spirited fisticuffs. The winner is the one who manages to drive the other back the length of three city blocks and into the open manhole at the end of his side of the screen. Meanwhile, both of you have to dodge the flower pots irate apartment dwellers occasionally heave down at you.

Layout: There are four screens: the block in the center where the fight begins (the Snack Bar), a block to the right of it (the Bookstore), and another to the right of that (the Barber Shop), which ends in an open manhole. To the immediate left of the Snack Bar is the Discount Shop, and to the left of that a Restaurant, which also ends with an open manhole.

Scroll: Side to side.

Hero's Powers: You have four different kinds of punches: slow but strong to the face or belly, and fast but weaker to the face or belly. Defensively you can use your hands to protect your face or belly; you can also "dodge," ducking your body backward to avoid blows. Obviously, the combatants can walk from side to side.

Hero's Weaknesses: Every punch you give or take robs you of stamina; a flower pot not only weakens you, but leaves you dazed. During this time your adversary can sneak in a punch.

About Your Enemies: Your opponent has the same powers and weaknesses as you.

Menu: You can fight the computer-controlled thug (on the right), or you can battle another player.

Timer: A fight on each block can last a maximum of 100 time units (3 minutes 28 seconds).

Scoring: Each player starts with 3 "lives," each possessing 200 stamina points. These are replenished each time a life is lost (that is, the fight moves onto a new block). They are drained according to the blow used: the fast punch costs you 1 point to deliver, 4 to take; and the hard blow costs 2 points to give and 10 to take. A hit from a flower pot costs 5 points, plus whatever damage your opponent does while you're watching the birdies (there's only enough time to toss one punch). If no one has won when time runs out, a police car takes away the fighter with the lowest stamina count.

Patterns: The player on the left only gets knocked to the left, and vice versa. There is no pattern to the dropping of the flower pots.

Beginner's Strategy: Although there is no advantage pointwise, most players tend to throw (and expect) punches to the head. Thus, a body-blow strategy, with occasional shots to the face, tends to throw other players off. Overall, always use a 1-2 tactic: a hard shot followed by a soft shot. Players who have just taken a punch tend to go into a defensive mode; don't waste the stamina on throwing a power punch, which in all likelihood will be blocked. When playing the computer, it can usually be lured under a flower pot if you duck.

Advanced Strategy: Work out combinations. For example, most players will move in on you if you duck back. They'll get confident if you then duck back again. They'll move in, and when they do, prepared to strike, they'll be unprotected. Thus, use a duck, duck, hard-blow combination. Most players also anticipate that opponents will use 2-1 blows: 2 shots to the head or belly, then switch. A 4-1 flurry usually catches them off-guard. On the defensive, try to rely on ducking. If you're in close and lower your guard to throw a punch, chances are better you'll get clocked. If you're out of range, there's nothing your opponent can do except take a step forward—in which case you'll greet them with a knuckle sandwich to the gut.

Par: A good fighter will use just 70 stamina points against the computer and slightly under 40 time units for each bout.

NES Advantage: No help.

Training Tips: Play a two-player game with one player. Set up the opposing fighter in different positions—face protected, belly protected, etc.—and practice adjusting quickly from facial punches to belly blows. Also in this mode, don't even bother with the other pugilist; just go over your own moves —especially the combinations.

Rating: This game isn't nearly as cathartic as *Kung Fu* or other hand-to-hand matches. There simply aren't enough options. Because of that, it also won't take you long to master. If flower pots fell more quickly than one or 2 per block, the game would have been much more exciting.

Challenge: C

Graphics: C

Sound Effects: C

CHAPTER TWENTY-NINE

WORLDRUNNER

Type: Science fiction quest.

Objective: The 8 worlds of solar system number 517 are being bullied by Grax and his vile Serpentbeast brothers. You are the hero who must run from world to world, blasting the invaders as well as the indigenous killers. Apart from monsters, the main obstacles in your adventure are huge, rectangular pits that cover the entire screen from left to right and must be leaped. These vary in width and in the distances between them.

Layout: Each of the 8 worlds is different and exotic. The horizon of each never changes as you run toward it (unless you shift from side to side). The ground rolls toward you, as do the huge pits and many monsters. The 8 worlds are Uno, Toro, Caverno, Quanto, Temero, Aquo, Invinso, and Fino.

Scroll: Your vantage point is from just over the runner's shoulder. The terrain unfolds *at* you; you can move from side to side.

Hero's Powers: Your hero begins the game with 3 lives. At the start he has nothing more than the ability to run, slow down, and make modest-sized jumps. However, as he acquires certain objects (which are either lying about or are hidden inside silvery columns), his talents increase: Laser Missiles allow you to fire destructive blasts; Power Potions enable you to survive one impact with an enemy; Atomic Power makes you invulnerable . . . but just for 5 seconds; Hearts give you an extra life; Cosmic Clocks replenish your power supply; Junior Jumpers give your leaps added boost; and Super Jumpers allow you to vault even farther. Though powers can be layered one on top of the other—for example, you can have Laser Missiles and Atomic Power at the same time—they are not cumulative. Even if you've gathered three Laser Missiles, that doesn't increase your firepower. Also, although a Power Potion will save you if you are hit by an enemy, the collision will cost you any other powers you've acquired.

Hero's Weaknesses: Colliding with most enemies, or falling into a pit, costs you a life. The exception is hitting a Hand Man (see About Your Enemies), which prevents you from moving ahead and thus drains you of strength. Also, repeated collisions with columns saps the hero's powers. Your runner has the ability to slow, but not to stop.

About Your Enemies: Instead of concealing Laser Missiles or Atomic Power, some columns contain Magic Mushrooms. These are instantly fatal. The roaming creatures you must face in turn are: Menacing Meanies, green orbs that roll toward you and from side to side; the White Willies, which do that and also bounce; the Robot Heads, which are faster, more plentiful versions of the meanies; the Towering Infernos, pillars of fire that don't move, but tend to appear right smack in your way when you're coming down on the other side of a pit; the Hand Men, which shift from side to side and leap to keep you back; Venus Die Traps, lethal roving flowers; Sea Shells; hero-eating Calamitous Clams; hero-seeking Spinners; the invincible Dog Face; the small but toxic Vapor Clouds; the winged Mean TV; and the indestructible Diamond Demons. Upon reaching the end of each world, you'll face one or more Serpentbeasts, depending upon how far along you are in the game. These slither and writhe from the horizon, their awesome jaws ready to devour you. The most formidable of these monsters, Grax, lurks on the eighth world. Lastly, there are the pits, which appear in every world and vary in width and proximity to one another.

Menu: There are 2-D and 3-D modes, which are exactly the same game. Players can switch from one to the other at any point in a game.

Timer: There is no timer; the hero must reach certain thresholds before his power runs out.

Scoring: Each time you defeat an enemy or scoop up a Star, you are awarded points. Any time you collect power-enhancers (Laser Missiles, Potions, etc.), you get points starting with the *second* one you grab in any given row. (This does *not* apply when you break up the collection. For example, if you find a row of columns where there are Laser Missiles, and you get only *one* Missile, you don't get points for the next Missile or Potion you nab in a *different* row.) There are also Warp Balloons floating about. Grabbing these carries the hero to another dimension, where he is allowed to roam menace-free for a time, collecting power boosters, Hearts, and so on.

Patterns: The scenery and approach of enemies and pits is the same each time you play the game. For example, on world number one, Uno, there are always Laser Missiles in the first row of columns, Power Potions in the second row, and Magic Mushrooms in the third. Moreover, there are 4 of each in every row. The first Warp Balloon can be found after the first 4 Stars (3 Hearts in a straight line, then one diagonally to the right). If you grab it, then follow the Stars in the new dimension, you'll encounter columns containing, first, a Power Potion, and next, a Heart. Among your enemies, the Clams move in circles.

Beginner's Strategy: To begin with, as soon as your runner appears, line him up with the seam between the two buildings on the horizon. You'll run right into a Laser Missile column. Hit it *twice*, the first time to get the Missile, the second time to bounce back so you can shift left and hit another column to get another Missile. You should collect a total of 4 Missiles in this fashion. Slide around the last of the columns and repeat this procedure with the Potion columns. (Hitting the columns costs you power, but the game will replenish it before you really need it.) When you run for the first pit, push the controller to the left. Since the runner goes forward by himself, this maneuver will carry you diagonally on the path that will give you the most Meanies to kill.

On any level be especially careful when jumping pits. Some of them have only narrow bands of land between them. A hefty jump will not only carry you over the pit, but over the land as well and send you plunging to your death in the next pit. If you're in the middle of a jump and you see land approaching rapidly, shift the controller to the left so you'll move diagonally. This will burn up most of the extra inertia and keep you on land. Also use this maneuver to avoid a Towering Inferno or Robot Head that may be waiting for you. On Toro you'll find that you won't be running and jumping, per se, but hopping over the closely-spaced pits. When racing through the White Willies, get between two columns of them and dart from side to side, plugging them. If you run directly toward them, chances are you'll get mashed. When you reach the Serpentbeast on any level, dash to the sides when it nears and keep blasting its head. For bigshot invaders, they're not as tough as you'd think. (Note: You don't need Lasers to kill them. You are armed automatically as soon as they approach.) When you reach Hand Men, begin your attack by taking long, high leaps diagonally to the left. This will enable you to clear them. When that no longer works, follow the Stars through the Hands (the Hands don't go near them). Whenever there are no Stars, run near, or even better, *between* the Towering Infernos. The Hands don't go near these either. In general, each time you leap a pit, you should land with your Laser Missiles blazing. You never know what may creep up suddenly. Scattershooting is actually recommended after a jump, since chances are good you won't have time to aim before you have to get ready to leap the next pit. Don't pass up any chance to get a Laser Missile: You'll need them! Also, be aware that if you reach one of the later worlds and lose your last life, you needn't go back to the first world. Just hold down button A and tap Start. The game will resume on the world where you left off (though you will be score-naked).

Advanced Strategy: Starting with Caverno, things really be-

141

gin to heat up. As soon as you arrive, use the controller to scroll the horizon from side to side until you see the 2 huge flowers bending toward each other. Line up your runner between these. When you reach Junior Jumpers (either on the land or in the pits), take your hands off the controller and let the Jumpers hurl you from one to the other. The only adjustments you'll need to make are when Towering Infernos appear. When these loom, simply hop to the row on the left or right. After the Inferno passes, get back in line with the two flowers: This is the row with the fewest number of Towering Infernos. Halfway through the world you'll begin reaching massive pits that have no Junior Jumpers until halfway across. To reach these, you'll have to use your controller to jump when you reach the pit, then use it again when you land on the Jumper. Together they'll give you a leap sufficient to reach land.

Par: To begin with, you should start the game with 3000 points just from collecting all the Laser Missiles and Power Potions. An average of 90,000 points on each world is good. (This tally is slightly misleading, however, since even a sub-par player can get it on Uno and a few other worlds. When you lose your first or second life, you don't lose your score. You go back to the beginning and, thus, get another shot at the Warp Balloon—which gives you access to hundreds of additional points.)

NES Advantage: Since the jumps require precision maneuvering, the joystick is a distinct advantage. The game has problems holding the image with slow motion. (Note: With either controller, when you press Pause, the runner sits down, facing you, and starts breathing heavily. A nice touch!)

Training Tips: Go through the game without collecting any powers; just practice jumping the pits and dodging enemies. Those skills will serve you better than firing (since many monsters come at you from the sides, where your laser fire is useless).

Rating: Not only isn't the 3-D version effective, it's often extremely distracting—especially when the two separate images don't quite come together and you feel like you're fighting doubles of every enemy! Stick to the 2-D version, which is *excellent*. Even after you've learned the patterns, getting *all* the Super Stars and shooting *every* Willy or Robot Head is a task and a half.

Challenge: A+

Graphics: B (Though the scenery rolls by nicely, and the animation of the runner is impressive, there's a *lot* of image breakup; the animation of the Serpentbeasts, as well as the eerie terrains each inhabits, is nearly worth the price of admission.)

Sound Effects: C— (Not much, apart from the music—though the Serpentbeast sounds are neat.)

CHAPTER THIRTY
ZELDA II
– THE ADVENTURE
OF LINK

Type: Fantasy quest.

Objective: In the world of long ago, Link—young hero of *The Legend of Zelda*— is now a strapping sixteen years old. And once again he sets out on a great adventure: this time to liberate Princess Zelda from an enchantment cast by his old nemesis, the heartless Prince of Darkness, Ganon. To accomplish this he must collect Keys placed in enchanted Crystals in the heads of the Stone Statues which lie in the depths of 6 dreary Palaces.

Layout: Pictured are the fields, swamps, mountains, ruins, forests, towns, dungeons, palaces, and labyrinths through which Link must travel.

Scroll: There are a few places in which Link goes up and down. For the bulk of the game, however, Link moves from side to side.

Hero's Powers: Once again setting out with modest abilities in the categories of Attack, Magic, and Life, Link can boost these strengths by picking up a Shield, Fire, Spells, Thunder, Jumping Ability, Reflections to cause spells to hurt whoever cast them, extra Life, Fairies who bestow wings, a Power Glove for breaking stone, a Magic Candle to see concealed objects, a Raft, Magic Boots, and an Enchanted Recorder whose notes funnel powers to Link by causing rifts in the realm.

Hero's Weaknesses: Link loses units of Life by being shot or stabbed by monsters, falling off collapsing bridges, being hit on the head with crumbling stone, and so forth.

About Your Enemies: Each step of the way is haunted by dangerous types. Among the most intimidating are the dog-faced, spear-wielding Molblin (who is much stronger now than in the previous game); the horse-headed Mazura and his mace; the not-very-good knight Rebonack and his iron steed; the helmeted Jermafenser; and, most iniquitous of all, the giant blue goblin Ganon.

Menu: There is only the one mission.

Timer: None. The game continues until Link cannot.

Scoring: Link obtains additional powers for objects he uncovers.

Patterns: Hyrule and environs, and most of the objects therein, are the same in every game.

Beginner's Strategy: Before you reach any palaces, as well as during your journey, you should tour a bit, going to villages and engaging people in conversation. Don't take what they say at face value. Sometimes people need to be questioned more than once before they'll part with the truth! For instance: Since you will be heading to the northern desert first, to enter Parapa, stop in Rauru and chat with an elderly gentleman to learn the Spell of the Shield. Afterward, to begin the quest proper, you must journey to the western regions of Hyrule, where you will obtain Heart Containers and Magic Jars. These are needed to help you survive your quest. The first Palace—Parapa—is located in the northeast corner of the kingdom and is especially rich in goods. To get around therein, descend after the first 4 columns, then head left. After you pass 6 columns and a ledge, a Key will be at the second ledge. At the other end of this level you'll find a Fairy. Backing up, past the column to your left, you'll be able to ascend to a level where you'll find another Key on the far right. Returning to the passage up and heading back to the second level, go left to the next passage. Descend and go left. At the very end of the corridor is a Candle. (Be careful: the bridge that lies between the stairs and the Candle is fragile. If you don't cross in a hurry, it'll crumble, and you're doomed.) When you have the Candle, go right. Return to the second level, head for the passage, and descend one level. On the right (past Mazura, who will greet you by the columns), is the Stone Statue where you must place a Crystal. When you meet Mazura, stay to the far left of the screen, duck to avoid his crunching mace, then leap and strike at his head. Finished here, head to the western central portion of the kingdom to find the Palace of Midoro. Upon arriving, walk to the down-passage, beyond the columns, descend one level, travel all the way to the left, go down another level, and head right. Get the Fairy here, then go left; the Power Glove is at the far end. You'll need it to smash the Blocks that rain down in this Palace. Return to the passage, climb to the second level, head for the stairwell on the right, and go down to the third level. Obtain the Key on the far left, then go back to the passage. Venture down another level, get the Key on the far right, then retrace your steps to the passage on the left. Go down to the fourth level and head right. Beneath a ledge is a passage to the bottom level. There, beyond the columns (and Jermafenser) is the second Stone Statue. Jermafenser can be defeated . . . but only after you've jumped and used your sword to swat off his helmet.

Advanced Strategy: Next on your agenda is the Island Palace, located in the southeasternmost corner of Hyrule. (Get there by going, first, to the village of Mido to learn the route to the isle . . . and also to find a fencing master who will teach you the Underthrust manner of fighting, a skill you'll need to take on Rebonack and also to shatter the stones that surround the Keys.) This Palace is the least complex of all. Go right, descend through the passage, then go right again. A Key is at the end. Double back; the downward passage lies beneath the thin ledge to the left of the bust. Go down, head all the way to the left to get the next Key, go to the far right to get the Raft, then go left again to the passage that leads below (to the right of the bust). The Stone Statue (guarded by Rebonack) is at the far right. Ironnack can be approached (assuming you have the Shield) and slain if you *kneel* and push Link's blade through his throat. To battle Rebonack, you must first unseat him using the Underthrust move, employing it while leaping.

Par: Clearing the first 3 Palaces is a good day's work.

NES Advantage: The big help here is rapid thrusts of your sword, and other weapons, by holding down the button.

Training Tips: It goes without saying that you should make a map of Hyrule and each edifice you enter. Spend time exploring the kingdom before entering the Palaces.

Rating: This is a strong sequel to the original classic. Despite the familiarity of the characters and the weakness of the visuals (which are much too bright and cartoonlike for an *adventure*), the odyssey is exciting . . . the more so if you never played the first game.

Challenge: A
Graphics: C
Sound Effects: B